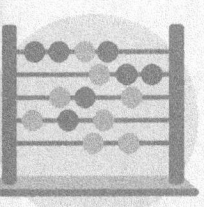

ACT Aspire TEST PREP

GRADE 3

MATH

Origins Publications

We help students develop their higher-order thinking skills while also improving their chances of admission into gifted and accelerated-learner programs.

Our goal is to unleash and nurture the genius in every student. We do this by offering educational and test prep materials that are fun, challenging and provide a sense of accomplishment.

Please contact us with any questions.

info@originspublications.com

Copyright © 2018 by Origins Publications

Written and Edited by: ACT Aspire Review Team

All rights reserved. This book or any portion thereof may not be reproduced or used in any manner whatsoever without the express written permission of the publisher.

ISBN 13: 978-1-948255-11-0

ACT Aspire is a registered trademark of ACT,Inc, which is not affiliated with Origins Publications. Act Aspire or ACT, Inc have not endorsed the contents of this book.

Origins Publications
New York, NY, USA
Email:info@originspublications.com

TABLE OF CONTENTS

Introduction 4
How To Use This Book 5
Test Prep Tips 6

Operations and Algebraic Thinking 7
Understand Multiplication (3.OA.A.1) 8
Understand Division (3.OA.A.2) 12
Use Multiplication & Division To Solve Word Problems (3.OA.A.3) 16
Find Unknown Values In Multiplication/Division Equations (3.OA.A.4) 19
Know and Use Properties of Multiplication & Division (M3.OA.B.5) 24
Find Unknown Factors: Division (3.OA.B.6) 29
Know Relationship between Multiplication & Division (3.OA.C.7) 33
Solve Two-Step Word Problems (3.OA.D.8) 37
Identify & Understand Arithmetic Patterns (3.OA.D.9) 41

Number and Operations In Base Ten 45
Round Whole Numbers (3.NBT.A.1) 46
Add & Subtract Whole Numbers (3.NBT.A.2) 49
Multiply Multiples of Ten (3.NBT.A.3) 52

Number and Operations-Fractions 55
Identify & Understand Fractions (3.NF.A.1) 56
Represent & Understand Fractions on a Number Line (3.NF.B.2) 59
Compare Fractions (3.NF.B.3) 64

Measurement and Data 69
Tell Time & Solve Word Problems Involving Time Intervals (3.MD.A.1) 70
Estimate & Measure Liquid Volume & Mass (3.MD.A.2) 76
Draw Scaled Picture & Bar Graphs & Solve Problems (3.MD.D.3) 80
Measure Lengths & Create Line Plots (3.MD.B.4) 90
Recognize Area (3.MD.C.5) 97
Measure Area (3.MD.C.6) 101
Relate Area to Multiplication & Addition (3.MD.C.7) 107
Solve Problems Involving Perimeter (3.MD.D.8) 114

Geometry 120
Recognize & Understand Shape Categories & Attributes (3.G.A.1) 121
Partition Shapes & Represent Parts as Fractions (3.G.A.2) 126

Answer Key and Explanations 131

Practice Tests 164
Practice Test One 165
Practice Test One Answer Key & Explanations 179
Access to Bonus Practice Test Two 183

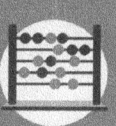

INTRODUCTION

The ACT Aspire

The ACT Aspire assessments are designed to measure whether students are meeting the rigorous Common Core State Standards that have been implemented in schools across America. These standards, or learning goals, outline what students in each grade should learn each year. These standards emphasize just how important the new goals are: they can help show whether students are on the right track to college and beyond, even when the students are years from those life stages.

ACT Aspire Mathematics Assessment

The ACT Aspire mathematics assessment is designed to determine whether students have mastered grade level appropriate mathematics skills. Like the Common Core State Standards, ACT Aspire assessments focus on higher level critical thinking skills, problem solving, analysis, and real-world application.

The ACT Aspire math assessments are given to students in in grades 3-10. The assessments are administered in a computer-based format, with paper-based format for students with special circumstances.

Each ACT Aspire math assessment for Grade 3-5 consists of one 55-minute session.

Question Format on ACT Aspire Math Assessments

Students taking the ACT Aspire mathematics assessment may be asked to respond to several types of questions. These include:

Selected response questions. These can require a *single answer,* where students select the correct response from four answer choices, or *multiple answers,* where a student must select a specified number of answers that s/he thinks best responds to the question.

Constructed response. Student is expected to produce a text or numerical response and/or explain or justify their answers and/or strategies in one or two complete sentences within the space, usually an answer box.

Technology enhanced items include questions that may ask students to drag and drop items, plot points on a number line, draw objects, complete a chart or graph, etc.

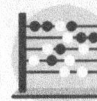

HOW TO USE THIS BOOK

The objective of this book is to provide students, educators, and parents with practice materials focused on the core skills needed to help students succeed on the ACT Aspire mathematics assessment.

A student will fare better on an assessment when s/he has practiced and mastered the skills measured by the test. A student also excels when s/he is familiar with the format and structure of the test. This book helps students do both. Students can review key material by standard through doing the skill-building exercises, as well as take practice tests to become accustomed to how the content is presented and to enhance test-taking skills. By test day, students will feel confident and be adequately prepared to do his or her best.

This Book Includes:

- 300 skill-building exercises organised by standard in order to help students learn and review concepts in the order that they will likely be presented in the classroom. These worksheets also help identify weaknesses, and highlight and strengthen the skills needed to excel on the actual exam. A variety of question types are included in the worksheets to help students build skills in answering questions in multiple formats, so they don't get tripped up by perplexing or unfamiliar question types on test day.

- Practice test materials that are based on the official ACT Aspire mathematics assessments released by the test administrator, and include similar question types and the same rigorous content found on the official assessments. By using these materials, students will become familiar with the types of items (including TEIs presented in a paper based format) and response formats they may see on the test. One ACT Aspire practice test is included in the book. **Another practice test can be downloaded as a PDF online. You will find instructions on accessing this test on page 184.**

- Answer keys with detailed explanations to help students not make the same mistakes again. These explanations help clear up common misconceptions and indicate how students might arrive at an answer to a question.

- Answer keys that also identify the standard/s that the question is assessing. If a student is having difficulty in one area, encourage the student to improve in that area by practicing the specific set of skills in the workbook.

- Test prep tips to help students approach the test strategically and with confidence.

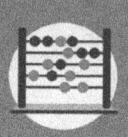

TEST PREP TIPS

First of all, remind your student to pay attention in class throughout the year, asking questions as needed on homework and classwork. The curriculum should follow the exact standards and skills that will be tested on the end-of-year assessment.

Another extremely effective strategy is to practice, practice, practice. Have your student work on practice questions and complete several full length practice tests. Our practice tests are a great place to start.

However, simply answering the questions and then moving on will not yield much improvement. If your student misses a question, discuss why the correct answer is indeed correct. Come up with alternate approaches to this question type that may work better in the future. Have your student explain his or her answer to each question. This gives you the opportunity to reinforce logical thinking and correct misconceptions as needed.

Prior to the test, encourage your student to get a solid night of sleep and eat a nourishing breakfast.

For children, avoiding test anxiety is very important, so be sure to avoid over-emphasizing the test or inadvertently causing a student to feel excessive stress or pressure.

In addition, **teach students general test-taking strategies such as the following:**

If you get stuck on a question, skip it and come back to it after answering easier questions.

There is no penalty for incorrect answers, so answer every question, even if you ultimately have to guess. On multiple choice questions, a 25% chance of answering correctly is still much better than no chance.

Don't panic when you get stuck on a question. Take a deep breath and remember that you are intelligent and prepared. No one is expected to answer every single question correctly.

Write out problems, create charts and graphs, or draw pictures and diagrams as necessary on scratch paper. Do whatever you think will help you visualize and correctly solve the problem.

If you follow the tips here, your student should be well on her way to a stress-free and successful performance on this important assessment.

OPERATIONS AND ALGEBRAIC THINKING

 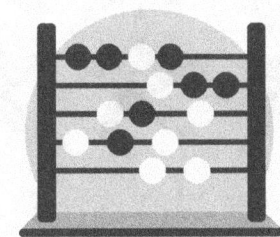 

       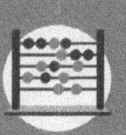  

UNDERSTAND MULTIPLICATION

3.OA.1.1 Interpret products of whole numbers, e.g., interpret 5 x 7 as the total number of objects in 5 groups of 7 objects each. For example, describe a context in which a total number of objects can be expressed as 5 x 7.

1. Circle the equation that that could be used to find the total number of stars.

    A. 3 + 3 = N
    B. 9 x 3 = N
    C. 3 x 3 = N
    D. 3 x 1 = N

2. The desks in the classroom are arranged in 4 rows with 6 desks in each row. Which **THREE** of the following equations could be used to find the total number of desks?

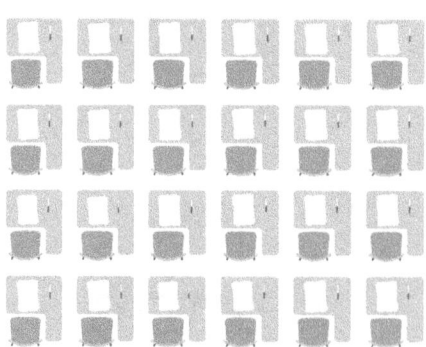

    ☐ 4 + 4 + 4 + 4 + 4 + 4 = 24 desks
    ☐ 6 + 6 + 6 + 6 = 24 desks
    ☐ 6 + 4 + 6 + 4 = 20 desks
    ☐ 4 x 6 = 24 desks

OPERATIONS & ALGEBRAIC THINKING

 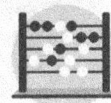        

3. Circle the product.

9 x 3 = N

    A. 27
    B. 3
    C. 6
    D. 12

4. Draw an array that can be used to find the product of 5 x 7 = N. Then find the product.

5 x 7 = N

N = _____

5. There are 3 bowls of bananas. Each bowl has 6 bananas. Which expression can be used to show the total number of bananas?
    A. 3 + 6
    B. 6 x 6 x 6
    C. 3 x 3 x 3 x 3 x 3 x 3
    D. 3 x 6

OPERATIONS & ALGEBRAIC THINKING

       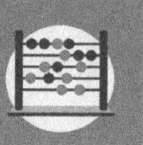 

6. There are 6 bookshelves. Each bookshelf has 7 books. Which **TWO** expressions can be used to show the total number of books?

    ☐ 6 + 7
    ☐ 6 x 7
    ☐ 7 x 7 x 7 x 7 x 7 x 7
    ☐ 7 + 7 + 7 + 7 + 7 + 7

    Explain how one of the expressions you selected can be used to help you find the total number of books on the bookshelves.

    _____

    _____

    _____

    _____

7. Erin is picking apples at the orchard. She has 2 barrels. If she puts 9 apples in each barrel, how many apples has she collected altogether? Use repeated addition to solve.

    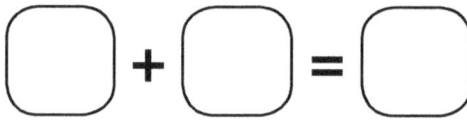

    Write a multiplication sentence to show many apples Erin collected altogether.

    _____

8. Danny runs 3 miles every day. How many miles does he run in 2 weeks?
    A. 21 miles
    B. 20 miles
    C. 6 miles
    D. 42 miles

9. Walter visited the zoo. His favorite animals were the elephants. How many elephants could he have seen if he saw between 35 and 40 legs altogether?
    Choose **ALL** possible choices.
    ☐ 10 elephants
    ☐ 8 elephants
    ☐ 9 elephants
    ☐ 7 elephants

10. Shane is having a lemonade stand. Each cup of lemonade costs 10 cents. How many cups of lemonade does Shane need to sell if he wants to make $5.00?
    A. 50 cups
    B. 5 cups
    C. 10 cups
    D. 100 cups

    After 2 days of selling lemonade, Shane made $3.50 cents. How many cups of lemonade did he sell after 2 days?
    A. 70 cups
    B. 7 cups
    C. 5 cups
    D. 35 cups

    How many more cups of lemonade does Shane need to sell until he meets his goal of $5.00?

    Answer = _____

11. The Patriots and Giants are playing each other in football. Each touchdown is worth 7 points. At the end of the game, the Patriots scored 8 touchdowns and the Giants scored 6 touchdowns. What was the final score of the game?
    A. Patriots- 8; Giants- 6
    B. Patriots- 56; Giants- 42
    C. Patriots- 15; Giants- 13
    D. Patriots- 50; Giants- 40

12. Richard is going on a road trip with his parents. To pass the time in the car, he counts the license plates of cars from other states. He saw 5 cars from New York, 5 cars from Connecticut, 6 cars from Florida, 1 car from California, and 1 car from Maine. If there are 4 wheels on each car, how many wheels did Richard see altogether?
    A. 18 wheels
    B. 72 wheels
    C. 22 wheels
    D. 24 wheels

    Richard also saw a couple of tractor trailers from other states. He saw 2 tractor trailers from Pennsylvania, 1 tractor trailer from Massachusetts, and 1 tractor trailer from Vermont. Each tractor trailer has 18 wheels. How many total wheels has Richard seen now?
    A. 72 wheels
    B. 18 wheels
    C. 16 wheels
    D. 144 wheels

OPERATIONS & ALGEBRAIC THINKING

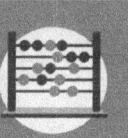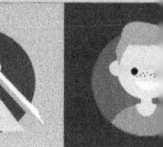

UNDERSTAND DIVISION

3.OA.1.2 Interpret whole-number quotients of whole numbers, e.g., interpret 56 ÷ 8 as the number of objects in each share when 56 objects are partitioned equally into 8 shares, or as a number of shares when 56 objects are partitioned into equal shares of 8 objects each.

1. Choose the equation that could be used to find how many equal groups of circles there are in the diagram below.

   A. 3 + 5 = N
   B. 5 + 5 + 5 + 5 + 5 = N
   C. 15 ÷ 5 = N
   D. 3 + 3 + 3 = N

2. Choose the equation that could be used to find how many hearts are in each group.

    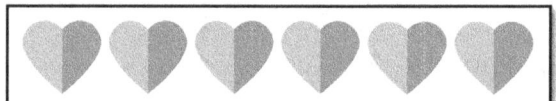

   A. 12 ÷ 2 = N
   B. 2 + 6 = N
   C. 2 + 2 = N
   D. 6 + 6 + 6 + 6 + 6 + 6 = N

3. Circle the quotient.

   $$6 ÷ 3 = N$$

   A. 3
   B. 6
   C. 9
   D. 2

OPERATIONS & ALGEBRAIC THINKING

4. Draw a model that can be used to find the quotient of 12 ÷ 3 = N
   Then find the quotient.

   12 ÷ 3 = N

   N = _____

5. The class has 40 slices of pizza. Each pizza has 8 slices. How many pizzas are there?
   - **A.** 48 pizzas
   - **B.** 5 pizzas
   - **C.** 8 pizzas
   - **D.** 32 pizzas

6. Grandma has 4 equal rows of tomato plants. She has 16 tomato plants altogether. Which **TWO** expressions can be used to show how many tomato plants are in each row?
   - ☐ 4 ÷ 16
   - ☐ 16 + 4 + 4 + 4 + 4
   - ☐ 16 ÷ 4
   - ☐ 16 − 4 − 4 − 4 − 4
   - ☐ 4 + 4 + 4 + 4

7. Andy has 63 pages left in his book. If he reads 9 pages a day, how many days will it take him to finish reading his book? Which expressions can be used to show many days it will take Andy to finish reading his book?
   - ☐ 63 ÷ 9
   - ☐ 63 − 9 − 9 − 9 − 9 − 9 − 9 − 9
   - ☐ 9 ÷ 63
   - ☐ 63 x 9
   - ☐ 9 x 63

   Choose an expression above to solve the problem. How many days will it take Andy to finish reading his book?

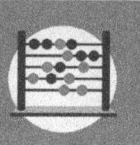

Answer: _____

8. Katie earns $5.00 for every chore she does. Yesterday, she earned $30.00. Which expression can be used to find out how many chores Katie did yesterday?

   A. 30 ÷ 5 =
   B. 5 ÷ 30 =
   C. 30 − 5 =
   D. 30 + 5 =

9. Jack has 132 pieces of Halloween candy. He keeps 22 pieces of candy for himself and shares the rest equally with 10 of his friends. How many pieces of candy will each friend get?

   A. 10 pieces of candy
   B. 22 pieces of candy
   C. 13 pieces of candy
   D. 11 pieces of candy

   Will Jack have any pieces of candy left over? Explain how you know.

   _____

   _____

   _____

10. Auntie Ava needs 32 eggs to make a breakfast platter. If eggs are sold in cartons of 12, how many cartons of eggs will Auntie Ava need to buy?

    A. 12
    B. 3
    C. 2
    D. 4

    How many eggs will Auntie Ava have leftover? _____

    Auntie Ava decides she wants to double the recipe. How many cartons of eggs will she need now?

    A. 6
    B. 5
    C. 8
    D. 12

11. 86 students and 7 adults went on a field trip to the zoo. If each van can hold 5 people, how many vans will they need?

    Answer: _____

    If each van costs $10 to rent for the field trip, how much will it cost altogether?

    Answer: _____

    When they got to the zoo, they had to pay $200 for admission. If each adult ticket costs $4.00, how much does each student ticket cost?

    Answer: _____

12. Mr. Clark had $100 to spend on 3 large pizzas for the family. After buying them, he had $55. How much did each pizza cost?

    Answer: _____

    Mr. Clark decided to buy ice cream cones with his leftover money. Each cone costs $4.00. If Mr. Clark buys 5 cones, how much money does he have leftover now?

    Answer: _____

    Does Mr. Clark have enough money left to buy $25 of gas for his truck?
    Explain how you know.

    _____

    _____

    _____

    _____

OPERATIONS & ALGEBRAIC THINKING

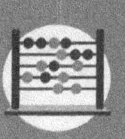

USE MULTIPLICATION & DIVISION TO SOLVE WORD PROBLEMS

3.OA.1.3 Use multiplication and division within 100 to solve word problems in situations involving equal groups, arrays, and measurement quantities, e.g., by using drawings and equations with a symbol for the unknown number to represent the problem.

1. Kim baked 3 batches of cookies. Each batch had 12 cookies. How many cookies did she bake altogether?
    - **A.** 4 cookies
    - **B.** 15 cookies
    - **C.** 36 cookies
    - **D.** 30 cookies

2. Jason wants to buy 5 pieces of candy. Each piece of candy costs 10 cents. Which number sentence could be used to find the total cost of the candy, c, in cents?
    - **A.** $10 \div 5 = c$
    - **B.** $10 \times 5 = c$
    - **C.** $10 + 5 = c$
    - **D.** $10 - 5 = c$

3. Colin has 72 tomato seeds. He wants to plant them in rows of 9. How many rows will he need to plant? Write your answer below using an equation with the unknown variable r for number of rows.

---

4. Lila is saving up for a new video game that costs $48. If she earns $6 a week for doing chores, how many weeks will she need to save before she can buy the video game?
    - **A.** 8 weeks
    - **B.** 54 weeks
    - **C.** 42 weeks
    - **D.** 6 weeks

5. Richard is putting photos in an album. The album has 11 pages. Each page can fit 4 photos. Which number sentence could be used to find the total number of photos, p, that Richard can fit in the album?
    - **A.** $11 + 4 = p$
    - **B.** $11 \div 4 = p$
    - **C.** $11 - 4 = p$
    - **D.** $11 \times 4 = p$

 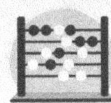        

6. Samantha is baking apple pies. She has 60 apple chunks. How many apple pies can Samantha make if she uses all the apple chunks?
    - **A.** 3 apple pies of 15 apple chunks each
    - **B.** 5 apple pies of 12 apple chunks each
    - **C.** 2 apple pies of 15 apple chunks each
    - **D.** 10 apple pies of 5 apple chunks each

7. The Miller Family was visiting the zoo. Each ticket costs $7. The Miller Family has 3 children and 2 adults. How much will it cost the family to go to the zoo?
    - **A.** $21
    - **B.** $35
    - **C.** $14
    - **D.** $12

8. The third grade class is having a pizza party. There are 21 students in the class. Each pizza has 9 slices. Emmi says the class will need 3 pizzas so that all students can have 1 slice. Is Emmi correct? Explain your thinking below.

_____

_____

_____

_____

_____

9. Omar bought 4 boxes of chocolate. Each box had 9 pieces of chocolate. Omar shared 12 pieces of chocolate with his friends. How many pieces of chocolate were left? Choose **ALL** equations that could be used to solve this problem, where 'c' represents pieces of chocolate.
    - ☐ (9 x 4) – 12 = c
    - ☐ (9 +4) – 12 = c
    - ☐ 13 – 12 = c
    - ☐ (9 x 4) + 12 = c
    - ☐ 36 – 12 = c

10. 26 girls and 22 boys are going on a field trip. Each van can hold 6 students. How many vans will they need for the field trip? Show how you can solve this problem in 2 different ways.

11. The Jackson Family is having a reunion. There will be 54 guests that can be seated at tables of 4 or tables of 6. How many tables will the Jackson Family need?
    A. 4 tables of 4 and 8 tables of 6
    B. 6 tables of 4 and 4 tables of 6
    C. 5 tables of 4 and 5 tables of 6
    D. 3 tables of 4 and 7 tables of 6

12. The school ordered construction paper for grades 3, 4, and 5. They ordered three packs of 24 sheets for grade 3, two packs of 12 sheets for grade 4, and two packs of 18 sheets for grade 5. How many sheets of paper did they order altogether?
    A. 144 sheets of paper
    B. 132 sheets of paper
    C. 54 sheets of paper
    D. 142 sheets of paper

 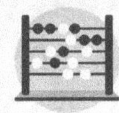        

FIND UNKNOWN VALUES IN MULTIPLICATION/DIVISION EQUATIONS

3.OA.1.4 Determine the unknown whole number in a multiplication or division equation relating three whole numbers.

1. Choose the correct number to complete the number sentence.

   2 x 4 = _____

   A. 8
   B. 6
   C. 4
   D. 2

2. Choose the correct number to complete the number sentence.

   3 x _____ = 15

   A. 12
   B. 3
   C. 5
   D. 3

OPERATIONS & ALGEBRAIC THINKING

3. Choose the correct number to complete the number sentence.

20 ÷ _____ = 4

   A. 4
   B. 20
   C. 16
   D. 5

4. Draw an array to solve the problem. Then solve.

30 ÷ 5 = N

N = _____

5. Choose the number that could make each of the statements below true.

21 ÷ N = 7   N x 4 = 12   N ÷ 1 = 3

   A. 2
   B. 6
   C. 3
   D. 9

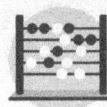

6. Complete the number sentence.

9 x N = 72

N = _____

7. Look at the table. Determine the rule and write it below. Then complete the table.

INPUT	4	5		7
OUTPUT	8		12	14

_____

_____

_____

8. Mom has 18 apples. She puts an equal number of apples in 3 pies. How many apples are in each pie? Choose the **TWO** expressions that could be used to solve this problem.
    - ☐ 3 ÷ 18
    - ☐ 18 ÷ 3
    - ☐ 3 x 6
    - ☐ 6 ÷ 3
    - ☐ 18 x 3

9. Complete the number sentence.

N ÷ 8 = 6

N = _____

Explain how multiplication can help you solve the problem above.

_____

_____

_____

OPERATIONS & ALGEBRAIC THINKING

10. What 3 numbers can be used to make the number sentence below true?

N x 6 = less than 30

    A. 5, 6, 30
    B. 2, 3, 4
    C. 4, 5, 6
    D. 5, 6, 7

11. Gabe is putting his baseball cards in an album. He can fit 5 or 6 baseball cards on a page. If Gabe has 90 baseball cards altogether, how many possible pages in the book can he use? Choose **ALL** answers that apply.
    ☐ 6
    ☐ 5
    ☐ 15
    ☐ 18

Gabe gets 30 new baseball cards for his birthday. He plans to put this baseball cards in the same album. How many more possible pages will Gabe need? Choose **ALL** answers that apply.
    ☐ 5
    ☐ 6
    ☐ 15
    ☐ 18

12. Armstrong Elementary School is having a fundraiser to raise money for a local dog shelter. They are selling 3 different kinds of cookies: Oatmeal Raisin, Peanut Butter, and Double Chocolate Chip.

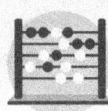

Max sold 4 Oatmeal Raisin Cookies and 5 Peanut Butter Cookies. How much money did he raise?

Answer: _____

Wendy only sold Double Chocolate Chip Cookies. She raised $32.00 How many cookies did she sell?

Answer: _____

Mrs. Miller loves Peanut Butter Cookies. She has $20. What is the greatest number of Peanut Butter Cookies she can buy?

Answer: _____

Explain how you know: _____

_____

_____

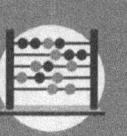

KNOW AND USE PROPERTIES OF MULTIPLICATION & DIVISION

3.OA.2.5 Apply properties of operations as strategies to multiply and divide (i.e.: commutative property of multiplication, associative property of multiplication, and distributive property).

1. Choose the correct number to complete the number sentence.

    5 x 4 = N x 5

    A. N = 20
    B. N = 5
    C. N = 4
    D. N = 40

2. Use the model below to find the product.

    (2 x 2) x 3 = N
    4 x 3 = N
    N =

    A. 12
    B. 7
    C. 4
    D. 3

24 — OPERATIONS & ALGEBRAIC THINKING

3. Draw a line to separate the triangles to match the equation. Then find the answer.

$3 \times 8 = N$

$(3 \times 2) + (3 \times 6) = N$

$N = $

- **A.** 11
- **B.** 6
- **C.** 18
- **D.** 24

4. Fill in the missing numbers to solve **2 x 4 x 5** in two different ways.

$2 \times 4 \times 5 = (2 \times 4) \times 5$

= ☐ x 5

= ☐

$2 \times 4 \times 5 = 2 \times (4 \times 5)$

= 2 x ☐

= ☐

5. Karen says that **5 x 0 = 5**. Is she correct? Explain how you know.

_____

_____

_____

_____

6. Choose TWO equations that can be used to solve the problem: **4 x 3 x 2**
   - ☐ 4 + (3 x 2)
   - ☐ (3 x 2) x 4
   - ☐ (4 x 3) x 2
   - ☐ 2 + (4 x 2)
   - ☐ (4 x 3) + 2

OPERATIONS & ALGEBRAIC THINKING

7. Which expression can be used to determine the total number of squares?

   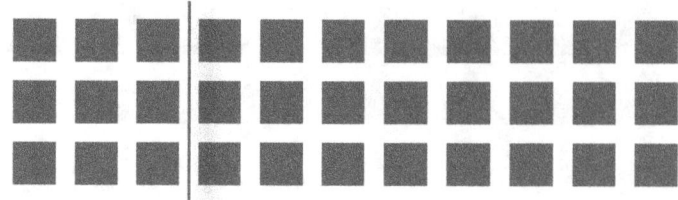

   A. 8 + 3 + 11
   B. 8 + (3 x 11)
   C. (8 + 3) + 11
   D. (3 x 3) + (3 x 8)

8. Alex says that the equations **27 ÷ 3 = 9** and **9 ÷ 3 = 27** mean the same thing because the commutative property says that you can change the order of the numbers and the answer will stay the same. Do you agree with Alex? Why or why not?

   _____

   _____

   _____

   _____

9. There are 2 bakers. Each baker has 3 trays. Each tray has 6 cookies. Choose the THREE expressions that could be used to show the total number of cookies.
   ☐ (2 x 3) x 6
   ☐ 2 + (3 x 6)
   ☐ 6 x 6
   ☐ 18 x 2
   ☐ (6 + 3) x 2

   How many cookies do the bakers have altogether?

   Answer: _____

10. Match each equation to the appropriate example of the distributive property.

9 x 7	(4 x 5) + (4 x 7)
6 x 8	(4 x 8) + (2 x 8)
4 x 12	(3 x 7) + (6 x 7)

11. Choose **ALL** the expressions that could be used to solve **6 x 7**.
    - ☐ 7 x 6
    - ☐ (2 x 3) x 7
    - ☐ (6 x 4) + (6 x 3)
    - ☐ 2 + (3 x 7)
    - ☐ 2 x (6 x 7)

   Choose one of the expressions you selected above. Explain how that expression could be used to solve **6 x 7**.

   _____

   _____

   _____

   _____

12. Mr. Jay has a large garden. The dimensions of his garden are below:

   He wants to split his garden up into 2 smaller sections so that he can separate his flowers and vegetables. Mr. Jay has 6 packages of flower seeds. Each package has between 15 and 20 seeds. He also has a box of vegetable plants arranged in 5 equal rows of 4.

   Draw a line to show a reasonable way Mr. Jay can split up his garden.

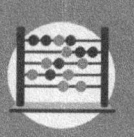

Mr. Jay wants to put up a fence around his garden to protect his flowers and plants. Choose an equation that can help Mr. Jay determine how much total fencing he will need.

- **A.** 18 x 7 x 18 x 17
- **B.** 18 ÷ 7
- **C.** 36 + 14
- **D.** 36 x 14

How much fencing will Mr. Jay need?

Answer: _____

Mr. Jay also wants to know the area of his garden so that he be sure his flowers and plants get enough water. Use what you know about the properties of multiplication to write an equation that could be used to find the total area of Mr. Jay's garden.

Equation: _____

Area: _____

 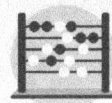        

FIND UNKNOWN FACTORS: DIVISION

3.OA.2.6. Understand division as an unknown-factor problem.

1. Use the picture to determine the missing number.

   $$10 \div 2 = N$$
   $$N \times 2 = 10$$

   N = _____

   A. 10
   B. 2
   C. 5
   D. 20

2. Which equation can be used to help solve for **21 ÷ 3 = N?**
   A. $3 \div 21 = N$
   B. $N \times 3 = 21$
   C. $21 \times 3 = N$
   D. $N \div 21 = 3$

3. Use the picture to determine the missing number.

   $$N \div 6 = 4$$
   $$6 \times 4 = N$$

   A. N = 24
   B. N = 6
   C. N = 20
   D. N = 4

4. Choose the number that would complete both number sentences.

$$35 \div N = 7$$
$$7 \times N = 35$$

   A. 7
   B. 35
   C. 3
   D. 5

5. 5 students are holding a bake sale. Each student needs to bake 12 cookies. Which number sentence could be used to show how many cookies they need to bake altogether?
   A. 5 × 12
   B. 60 × 12
   C. 60 ÷ 12
   D. 5 ÷ 12

6. Which number sentence is equivalent to the number sentence below?

$$4 \times N = 36$$

   A. 36 × 4 = N
   B. N + 4 = 36
   C. 36 ÷ 4 = N
   D. N ÷ 4 = 36

7. Abby wants to solve 42 ÷ 6, but she doesn't know all her division facts yet. Her friend, Ethan, tells her that she can use her multiplication facts to help her solve division problems. Explain how multiplication can help Abby solve 42 ÷ 6.

_____

_____

_____

_____

$$42 \div 6 = N$$

N = _____

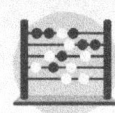

8. Draw a line to match each division equation on the left with its inverse multiplication equation on the right.

$24 \div 3 = 8$ $12 \times 3 = 36$
$24 \div 6 = 4$ $8 \times 3 = 24$
$20 \div 5 = 4$ $12 \times 2 = 24$
$36 \div 3 = 12$ $4 \times 5 = 20$
$24 \div 2 = 12$ $4 \times 6 = 24$

9. Which of the following equations **cannot** be used to solve $28 \div 4 = N$?

   A. $28 \div N = 4$
   B. $4 \times N = 28$
   C. $N \times 4 = 28$
   D. $4 \div N = 28$

   Explain why the equation you chose cannot be used to solve $28 \div 4 = N$.

   _____
   _____
   _____
   _____

10. 9 students are working on a class project. Each student needs 6 cotton balls, 2 paper bags, 4 straws, and 9 paper plates. Which number sentence can be used to find the total number of paper plates the students will need?

    A. $9 \times 9 = N$
    B. $9 \div 9 = N$
    C. $N \div 9 = 9$
    D. $9 \div N = 9$

    How many paper plates will the students need altogether?

    Answer: _____

OPERATIONS & ALGEBRAIC THINKING

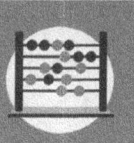

A student counted 34 straws. Are there enough straws for each student? Yes or no?

Answer:_____

Use a division and a multiplication number sentence to explain how you know.

Division number sentence: _____

Multiplication number sentence: _____

11. Drew said that he doesn't need to memorize any division facts. He said that if he knows his multiplication facts, he also knows his division facts. Do you agree with Drew? Use an example of a division fact and a multiplication fact to support your answer.

_____

_____

_____

12. The Shu Family is having a wedding. 52 guests plan on attending. 4 guests can sit at a square table, 6 guests can sit at a rectangular table, and 10 guests can sit a circular table. How many of each type of table might the Shu Family need so that all guests have a seat and there are no extra seats?

_____ square tables

_____ rectangular tables

_____ circular tables

The Shu Family wants to make sure that there are enough desserts so that each person can have 2. Which number sentence can be used to determine how many desserts they will need altogether?

    A. $52 \div 2 = N$
    B. $2 \div 52 = N$
    C. $52 \times N = 2$
    D. $52 \times 2 = N$

How many desserts will the Shu Family need altogether?
Answer?_____

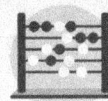

KNOW RELATIONSHIP BETWEEN MULTIPLICATION & DIVISION

3.OA.3.7 Fluently multiply and divide within 100, using strategies such as the relationship between multiplication and division or properties of operations. By the end of grade 3, know from memory all products of two one-digit numbers.

1. Find the product. $0 \times 7 = N$

    N = _____

    A. 7
    B. 1
    C. 70
    D. 0

2. Find the quotient. $25 \div 5 = N$

    N = _____

    A. 5
    B. 25
    C. 10
    D. 1

3. Solve the equation. $3 \times 7 = N$

    N = _____

    A. 3
    B. 7
    C. 21
    D. 4

4. Solve. $N \div 2 = 10$

    N = _____

    A. 2
    B. 10
    C. 5
    D. 20

OPERATIONS & ALGEBRAIC THINKING

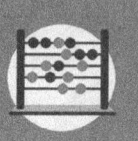

5. Match the multiplication sentence to the related division sentence.

   3 x 9 = 27   12 ÷ 2 = 6
   4 x 3 = 12   30 ÷ 10 = 3
   5 x 6 = 30   27 ÷ 3 = 9
   2 x 6 = 12   12 ÷ 4 = 3
   10 x 3 = 30   30 ÷ 5 = 6

6. Choose the number sentence that is needed to complete the fact family below.

   3 x 6 = 18
   18 ÷ 3 = 6
   6 x 3 = 18

   A. 18 ÷ 6 = 3
   B. 3 ÷ 6 = 18
   C. 6 ÷ 3 = 18
   D. 18 x 3 = 6

7. Find the quotient.

   0 ÷ 2 = N

   N = _____

   A. 0
   B. 2
   C. 1
   D. 20

8. Create a fact family using the digits 4, 8, 32.

   _____ x _____ = _____

   _____ x _____ = _____

   _____ ÷ _____ = _____

   _____ ÷ _____ = _____

9. Which expressions below have a product of 42? Choose **ALL** that apply.
   ☐ 6 x 7
   ☐ 14 x 3
   ☐ 21 x 2
   ☐ 42 x 0

10. Complete the chart below.

÷	9	18	27	36		
9						

Identify and explain 2 patterns that you notice in the table above.

_____

_____

_____

11. Kara went apple picking. Each basket had 7 apples. She collected 28 apples altogether. How many baskets does she have?
    - **A.** 7
    - **B.** 21
    - **C.** 3
    - **D.** 4

   Kara's brother also went apple picking. He has 5 baskets and each basket has 8 apples. How many apples does Kara's brother have?
    - **A.** 40
    - **B.** 3
    - **C.** 13
    - **D.** 45

   How many apples did Kara and her brother collect altogether?
    - **A.** 15
    - **B.** 35
    - **C.** 48
    - **D.** 68

12. James is saving for a new bike that costs $62.00. He earns $5.00 for each yard he rakes and he earns $4.00 each day he does his chores. James can rake up to 5 yards on the first day of the week, but none the rest of the week. If James already has $12.00, how many days will he need to work before he has enough money to buy a new bike?
    - **A.** 3
    - **B.** 6
    - **C.** 7
    - **D.** 8

Will James have any money left over? If so, how much money will he have left over? Explain how you know.

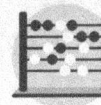

SOLVE TWO-STEP WORD PROBLEMS

3.OA.4.8 Solve two-step word problems using the four operations. Represent these problems using equations with a letter standing for the unknown quantity. Assess the reasonableness of answers using mental computation and estimation strategies including rounding.

1. Lila has 12 strawberries. She eats 2 and gives 3 to her baby sister. How many strawberries does Lila have left?

   $$12 - 2 = 10$$
   $$10 - 3 = s$$

   $s =$ _____

   A. 10
   B. 9
   C. 7
   D. 17

2. Brady picked 36 blueberries. He ate 6 and split the rest evenly between him and his 2 siblings. How many blueberries does each child get?

   $$36 - 6 = 30$$
   $$30 \div 3 = b$$

   $b =$ _____

   A. 30
   B. 27
   C. 6
   D. 10

3. The classroom has a box of 50 tissues. After 5 days, the box has 25 tissues left. How many tissues were used each day?

   What expression shows the first thing we need to solve in order to answer this question?
   A. $50 - 25 = t$
   B. $50 \div 25 = t$
   C. $50 - 5 = t$
   D. $50 \times 5 = t$

OPERATIONS & ALGEBRAIC THINKING

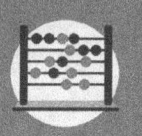

4. Mr. Watters picked the ripe vegetables from his garden. He picked some tomatoes, 10 cucumbers, and 6 peppers. He picked 28 vegetables in all. How many tomatoes did he pick?

   A. 16
   B. 12
   C. 28
   D. 14

5. Joe got $100 for his birthday. He bought new sneakers for $60.00 and candy for $12.00. Which expression can be used to show how much money (*m*) Joe had left over after shopping?

   A. 100 − 60 − 12 = *m*
   B. 60 + 12 − 100 = *m*
   C. 100 + 60 + 12 = *m*
   D. 100 + 60 − 12 = *m*

   Solve. How much money did Joe have left over after shopping?

   Answer: _____

6. Rob sent out 22 invitations for his party. His mom invited 3 more guests. If Rob wants each person to have 2 cupcakes, how many cupcakes will he need?

   A. 25
   B. 22
   C. 55
   D. 50

7. The Dolphins scored 4 touchdowns. Each touchdown is worth 7 points. They also scored 3 field goals. Each field goal is worth 3 points. Which expression can be used to show how many points (*p*) the Giants scored altogether?

   A. 7 + 3 = *p*
   B. 7 + 4 + 3 + 3 = *p*
   C. 7 × 4 + 3 × 3 = *p*
   D. 11 + 6 = *p*

   Solve. How many points did the Giants score altogether?

   Answer: _____

OPERATIONS & ALGEBRAIC THINKING

8. Rachel started reading a 325-page book on Monday. She read 12 pages on Monday, Tuesday, and Wednesday night. On Thursday she read 15 pages. Which expression can be used to show how many pages (*p*) are left in the book?

    A. 325 − 12 − 15 = *p*
    B. 12 + 15 + 325 = *p*
    C. 325 - 12 x 3 - 15 = *p*
    D. 325 − 12 x 15 = *p*

    Solve. How many pages are left in the book?

    Answer: _____

9. Muhammad is having a birthday party. He sent out 14 invitations and his mom sent out 9 more invitations. 2 people cannot come. How many guests (*g*) will be at his birthday party? Choose **ALL** the expressions that can be used to solve this problem?

    ☐ 14 + 9 − 2 = *g*
    ☐ 14 x 9 − 2 = *g*
    ☐ 23 + 2 = *g*
    ☐ 23 − 2 = *g*
    ☐ 14 + 9 ÷ 2 = *g*

    How many guests will be at Muhammad's birthday party?

    Answer: _____

    Muhammad wants each guest to have a goodie bag. Each goodie bag costs $2.00. How much money will the goodie bags costs altogether?

    Answer: _____

10. Liz wants to make s'mores. She has $30.00. Each bag of marshmallows costs $3.00, each box of crackers costs $2.00, and each candy bar costs $1.00. She needs to buy 2 bags of marshmallows, 2 boxes of crackers, and 10 candy bars. Does she have enough money? Explain how you know.

    _____
    _____
    _____

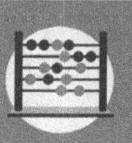

11. Elle has 25 baseball cards. Jake has twice as many baseball cards as Elle and Mark has 10 fewer baseball cards than Jake.

    How many baseball cards does Jake have? _____

    How many baseball cards does Mark have? _____

    How many more baseball cards does Mark have than Elle? _____

    How many baseball cards do Jake, Mark, and Elle have altogether? _____

12. Mrs. Winters is preparing to run a 15-mile marathon. For the first 10 days, she will run 3 miles a day. For the second 10 days, she will run 6 miles a day. For the third 10 days, she will run 9 miles a day. How many miles did Mrs. Winters run altogether in 30 days?

    Answer: _____

    If Mrs. Winters keeps running in this pattern, how many days will it take her to run 15 miles on a single day? Explain how you know.

    Answer: _____

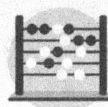

IDENTIFY & UNDERSTAND ARITHMETIC PATTERNS

3.OA.4.9 Identify arithmetic patterns, and explain them using properties of operations. For example, observe that 4 times a number can be decomposed into two equal addends.

1. Which rule describes the pattern shown?

    3, 6, 9, 12, 15

    A. × 3
    B. -3
    C. +3
    D. ÷3

2. Which of the following is an odd number?
    A. 345,679
    B. 269,780
    C. 553,764
    D. 915,128

3. Which of these sets does not contain any odd numbers?
    A. 23, 57, 69, 153
    B. 49, 87, 145, 217
    C. 22, 60, 110, 238
    D. 20, 45, 88, 95

4. Which of the following have an odd sum? Choose **ALL** that apply.
    ☐ 12 + 5
    ☐ odd number + odd number
    ☐ 7 + 7
    ☐ odd number + even number
    ☐ 15 + 5

5. Complete the statement. The sum of two even numbers will always be _____.
    A. Odd
    B. greater than 100
    C. less than 100
    D. even

OPERATIONS & ALGEBRAIC THINKING

6. Complete the table below.

Number of cars	3	4	5	6	7	8
Number of wheels	12	16		24		

Explain the rule in the table above.

_____

_____

_____

7. Complete the statement. The sum of an even number and an odd number will always

_____.

    A. be even
    B. be divisible by 2
    C. be a multiple of 4
    D. be odd

8. Complete the statement. The multiples of 5 will always _____.
    A. be odd
    B. be even
    C. have a 5 in the ones place
    D. none of the above

9. Circle the number that does not belong.

54, 60, 18, 9, 36, 45

Explain why the number you circled does not belong with the other numbers in the sequence.

_____

_____

_____

10. Jade knows all of her 4s times table. Malik tells Jade that if she knows her 4s facts, she can easily learn her 8s facts on the times table. Do you agree with Malik? Explain why or why not.

_____

_____

_____

11. Look at the multiplication table below.

X	0	3	4	5	6	7
3	0	9		15		21
4	0		16	20	24	28
5	0	15	20	25	30	35
6	0		24	30	36	
7	0	21		35		49

Which facts does this student seem to know well? Explain how you know.

_____

_____

Which facts does this student still need to practice? Explain how you know.

_____

_____

Fill in the missing numbers in the multiplication table.

       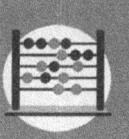  

12. What 3 numbers come next in the pattern?

     25, 28, 23, 26, 21, 24, 19, _____, _____, _____

   A. 17, 15, 13
   B. 24, 29, 34
   C. 14, 17, 12
   D. 22, 17, 20

Write the rule for the pattern above.

_____

_____

_____

Will one of the numbers in the above pattern ever be 0? Explain why or why not.

_____

_____

_____

_____

OPERATIONS & ALGEBRAIC THINKING

NUMBER AND OPERATIONS IN BASE TEN

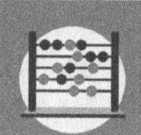

ROUND WHOLE NUMBERS

3.NBT.1.1. Use place value understanding to round whole numbers to the nearest 10 or 100

1. Use the number line below to round 34 to the nearest 10.

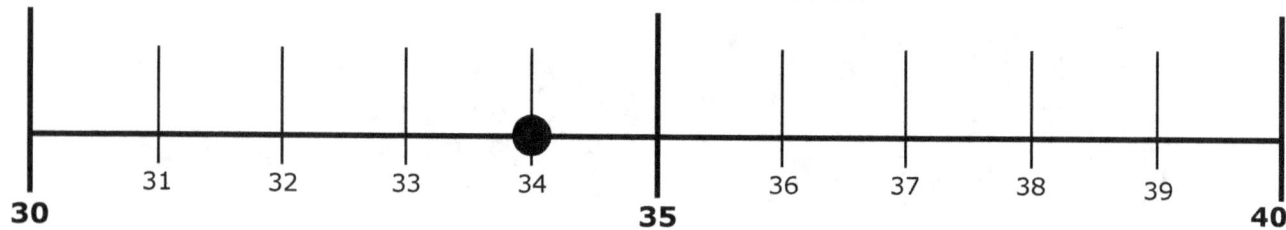

    A. 35
    B. 30
    C. 40
    D. 34

2. Use the number line below to round 256 to the nearest 100.

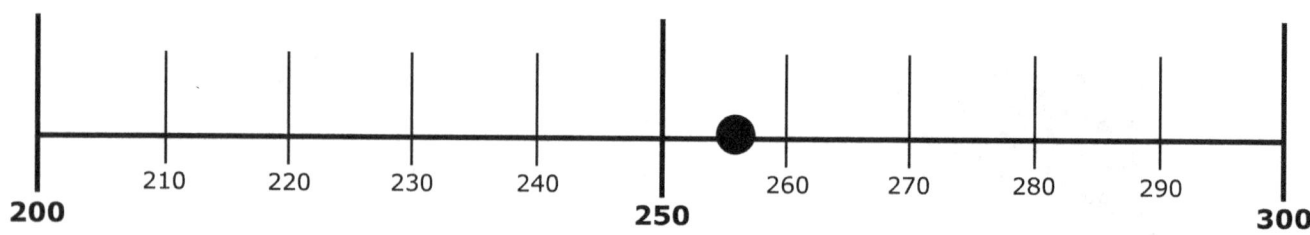

    A. 250
    B. 200
    C. 260
    D. 300

3. Complete the chart below.

Number	Round to the nearest 10	Round to the nearest 100
146		
375		
33		
286		

4. Which of the following numbers round to 100 when rounding to the nearest 100? Choose **ALL** answers that apply.
   - ☐ 50
   - ☐ 125
   - ☐ 150
   - ☐ 45
   - ☐ 85

5. Kemi is planning her birthday party. She needs to have enough brownies so that each guest can have 1 brownie. She is planning to have 17 guests. What is this number rounded to the nearest 10?
   - **A.** 10
   - **B.** 15
   - **C.** 0
   - **D.** 20

6. What is 1,056 rounded to the nearest 100?
   - **A.** 1,000
   - **B.** 1,100
   - **C.** 1,050
   - **D.** 1,060

7. When rounding to the nearest 10, which of the following numbers does **NOT** round to 10?
   - **A.** 5
   - **B.** 11
   - **C.** 15
   - **D.** 13

8. Emily says that when rounding to the nearest 100, 150 rounds down to 100.
   Is Emily correct? Explain your thinking below.

   _____

   _____

   _____

9. Which answer choice rounds each number in the equation below to the nearest 10 to find the sum?

   235 + 452 = N

   - **A.** 250 + 450 = 700
   - **B.** 200 + 500 = 700
   - **C.** 240 + 450 = 690
   - **D.** 235 + 455 = 690

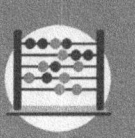

10. The Smith Family is planning a picnic. They are having 34 guests. They are planning for each guest to eat approximately 2 cookies. **About** how many cookies should they bake?
    A. 60 cookies
    B. 48 cookies
    C. 35 cookies
    D. 30 cookies

11. Chris collects sports cards. He has 117 baseball cards, 87 football cards, and 104 basketball cards. **About** how many sports cards does Chris have altogether? (*Hint: Use rounding/estimating to arrrive at your answer*).

    Show your work.

    _____

    _____

    _____

    _____

    Answer: _____

    For his birthday, Chris got 42 new sports cards. His friend Nick says that Chris now has about 350 sports cards altogether. Is Nick correct? Explain your thinking below.

    _____

    _____

    _____

12. Shawn went shopping for school supplies. He spent $4.50 on folders, $6.76 on writing utensils, and he bought a new backpack for $15.99. He paid with a $50.00 bill. **About** how much change should Shawn get back?
    A. $30.00
    B. $25.00
    C. $27.25
    D. $20.00

 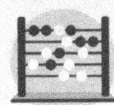        

ADD & SUBTRACT WHOLE NUMBERS

3.NBT.1.2. Fluently add and subtract within 1,000 using strategies and algorithms based on place value, properties of operations, and/or the relationship between addition and subtraction.

1. What expression shows the number 127 in expanded form?
   - **A.** 1 hundred, 2 tens, 7 ones
   - **B.** 100 − 20 − 7
   - **C.** one hundred twenty-seven
   - **D.** 100 + 20 + 7

2. What is the standard form of: 500 + 30 + 9?
   - **A.** 500, 309
   - **B.** 5,039
   - **C.** 539
   - **D.** 500, 039

3. Find the sum.

   $$\begin{aligned}50 \\ +\ 45\end{aligned}$$

   - **A.** 95
   - **B.** 105
   - **C.** 15
   - **D.** 55

4. Find the difference.

   $$\begin{aligned}417 \\ +\ 203\end{aligned}$$

   - **A.** 6,110
   - **B.** 217
   - **C.** 214
   - **D.** 204

5. Which **THREE** of the following expressions has the same difference as 50 − 35?
   - ☐ 50 + 35
   - ☐ 30 − 15
   - ☐ 45 − 30
   - ☐ 15 − 0

NUMBER AND OPERATIONS IN BASE TEN

6. Find the sum.

    392 + 618 = N

    N = _____

7. Jon pulled 485 seeds out of his pumpkin. Claire pulled 549 seeds out of her pumpkin. Which expression could be used to determine how many pumpkin seeds they had altogether?
    A. 485 × 549
    B. 549 − 485
    C. 549 ÷ 485
    D. 549 + 485

    Jon and Claire's mom baked 150 of their pumpkin seeds. How many pumpkin seeds are left?

    Answer: _____

8. Which of the following number sentences has a difference of 85?
    A. 100 + 85
    B. 100 − 85
    C. 135 − 50
    D. 185 − 85

9. Ana solved the following problem. 354 + 616 = 9,610. What mistake did Ana make?

    _____
    _____
    _____

    What is the correct sum for 354 + 616?
    A. 9, 610
    B. 610
    C. 961
    D. 970

 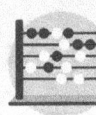        

10. Sam collected 293 stickers. His friend Abby gave him 150 more and his friend Helen gave him 89 more. Choose the **TWO** expressions that could be used to determine how many stickers Sam has altogether.

    ☐ 293 + 150 + 89
    ☐ 293 + 239
    ☐ 293 − 239
    ☐ 293 x 150 x 39

How many stickers does Sam have altogether?

Answer: _____

11. Luke has $50.00. He wants to buy a new video game for $19.99, a new book for $14.99, and a new shirt for $19.99. Does Luke have enough money? Explain how you know your answer is reasonable.

12. Write true or false. **The difference of 1,000 − 439 is less than 500.**

Charlie is having a hard time subtracting whole numbers with zeroes in them. Explain to Charlie how you would find the difference of: 1,000 − 439.

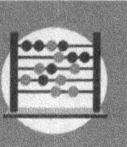

MULTIPLY MULTIPLES OF 10

3.NBT.1.3. Multiply one-digit whole numbers by multiples of 10 in the range 10-90 using strategies based on place value and properties of operations.

1. Find the product. **5 x 10 =?**
   - A. 1
   - B. 5
   - C. 50
   - D. 10

2. Find the product. **10 x 10 =?**
   - A. 1
   - B. 10
   - C. 0
   - D. 100

3. Find the product. **20 x 2 = ?**
   - A. 40
   - B. 10
   - C. 1
   - D. 20

4. Complete the statement. The product of 3 x 40 is _____.
   Choose **ALL** that apply.
   - ☐ greater than 100
   - ☐ an even number
   - ☐ 70
   - ☐ 120

5. Choose the **THREE** expressions that have the same product as **4 x 50.**
   - ☐ 50 + 50 + 50 + 50
   - ☐ 20 x 10
   - ☐ 4 + 4 + 4 + 4 + 4
   - ☐ 50 x 4

6. Alex gets $10 a week for allowance. He is saving up for a new baseball bat that costs $45.00. How many weeks will Alex have to save his allowance?
   A. 3
   B. 4
   C. 5
   D. 6

   Will Alex have any money left over? Explain how you know.

   _____

   _____

7. There are 20 students in a third-grade class going on a field trip to the farm. The bus costs $3 per student and tickets to the farm cost $4 per student. How much money will it cost the third-grade class to go to the farm?
   A. $140
   B. $80
   C. $60
   D. $200

8. Complete the table below by placing the correct number in the appropriate place.

INPUT	2	3	4			7
OUTPUT	160	240		400		

   Explain the rule that is shown in the table above.

   _____

   _____

   _____

9. Choose **ALL** the expressions that have a product greater than 200.
   ☐ 20 x 5
   ☐ 6 x 30
   ☐ 4 x 60
   ☐ 30 x 7

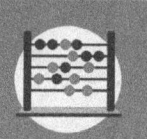

10. Explain how Mike can use 6 x 8 to help him solve 80 x 6.

   _____

   _____

   _____

   Solve for 80 x 6.
   - **A.** 806
   - **B.** 480
   - **C.** 48
   - **D.** 488

11. Decide if each statement is true or false. Write T if the statement is True. If the statement is false, write the correct answer on the line.

    30 x 100 = 300   _____

    50 x 4 = 200   _____

    240 ÷ 80 = 3   _____

    1,000 ÷ 50 = 5   _____

    20 x 800 = 1600   _____

12. Kevin has $40. He has twice as much money as his brother, Dan. Kevin's sister, Lauren, has four times as much money as Dan.

    How much money does Dan have? _____

    How much money does Lauren have? _____

    How much money do Kevin, Dan, and Lauren have altogether? _____

NUMBER & OPERATIONS - FRACTIONS

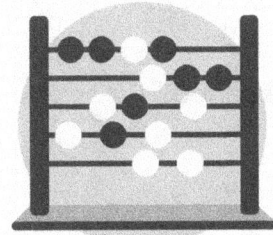

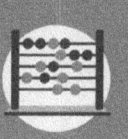

IDENTIFY & UNDERSTAND FRACTIONS

3.NF.1.1. Understand a fraction 1/*b* as the quantity formed by 1 part when a whole is partitioned into *b* equal parts; understand a fraction *a*/*b* as the quantity formed by a parts of size 1/*b*.

1. What fraction of the square is shaded?

   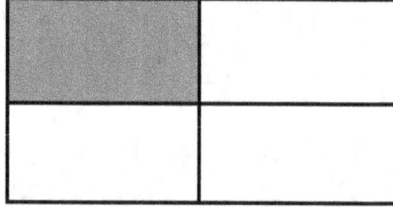

   A. $1/4$
   B. $4/4$
   C. $4/1$
   D. $3/4$

2. What fraction of the circle is shaded?

   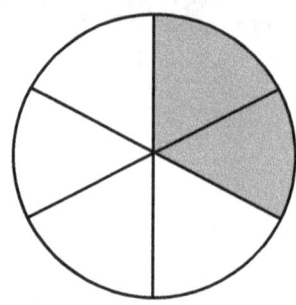

   A. $4/6$
   B. $2/4$
   C. $2/6$
   D. $4/2$

3. What fraction of the rectangle is shaded? Write your answer in the boxes below.

   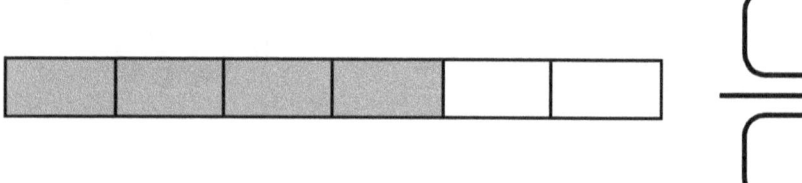

4. Shade the figures below to show the fraction $2/8$.

   Explain what the numerator and denominator tells you about the figures.

   _____

   _____

56 NUMBER & OPERATIONS – FRACTIONS

5. Look at the figures below. Circle the figures that are divided into sixths.

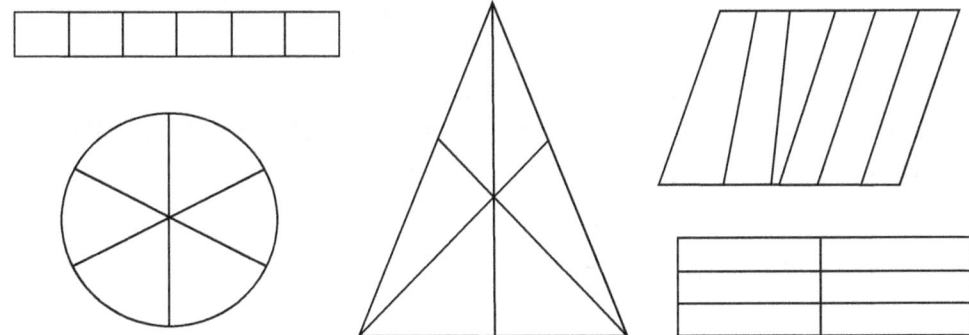

6. An apple pie is cut into 8 equal pieces. Chris ate 2 pieces. What fraction of the pie did Chris eat?
    A. 6
    B. 2
    C. $^6/_8$
    D. $^2/_8$

   What fraction of the pie did not get eaten?
    A. 6
    B. 2
    C. $^6/_8$
    D. $^2/_8$

7. What fraction of the rectangle is shaded? Choose the **TWO** answers that apply.

   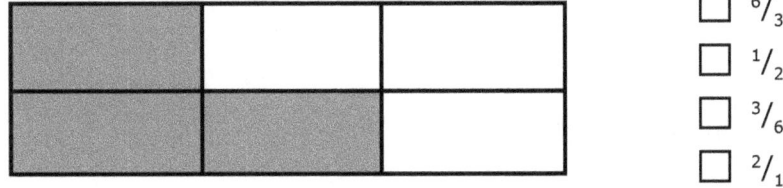

   ☐ $^6/_3$
   ☐ $^1/_2$
   ☐ $^3/_6$
   ☐ $^2/_1$

8. A pizza has 12 slices. 4 slices have pepperoni, 3 slices have meatball, and the rest of the slices have plain cheese. What fraction of the pizza was plain cheese?
    A. 5
    B. $^5/_{12}$
    C. $^{12}/_5$
    D. $^7/_{12}$

9. Alex has 6 blocks in his hand. 2 blocks are red, 1 block is black, and the rest are yellow. What fraction of the blocks is yellow? Choose the **TWO** answers that apply.
    ☐ $^3/_6$
    ☐ 3
    ☐ $^1/_2$
    ☐ $^6/_3$

NUMBER & OPERATIONS – FRACTIONS

10. 3 people are sharing 4 brownies. They want to split the brownies equally. How can they split the brownies equally? Choose **ALL** answers that apply.
    - ☐ It is not possible to split the brownies equally.
    - ☐ Cut each brownie into 3 equal pieces and pass them out equally.
    - ☐ Each person gets 1 whole brownie. Cut the last brownie into 3 equal pieces and give each person 1 piece.
    - ☐ Cut each brownie into 4 equal pieces and pass them out equally.

    If 3 people share 4 brownies equally, what portion of the brownies will each person get? Choose the **TWO** answers that apply.
    - ☐ $3/4$
    - ☐ $4/12$
    - ☐ $3/12$
    - ☐ $1\,1/3$
    - ☐ $1/3$

11. Dan went to the toy store with $24. He spent $1/4$ of his money. How much money did Dan spend?
    - **A.** $4
    - **B.** $12
    - **C.** $8
    - **D.** $6

    How much money does Dan have left?

    Answer: _____

12. A bake sale had 40 treats. One half of the treats sold in the morning and one fourth of the treats sold in the afternoon. What fraction of the treats were left at the end of the day?
    - **A.** one half
    - **B.** one fourth
    - **C.** three fourths
    - **D.** two fourths

    How many treats were left at the end of the day?
    - **A.** 5
    - **B.** 10
    - **C.** 15
    - **D.** 20

REPRESENT & UNDERSTAND FRACTIONS ON A NUMBER LINE

3.NF.1.2. Understand a fraction as a number on the number line; represent fractions on a number line diagram.

1. What fraction does the number line show?

   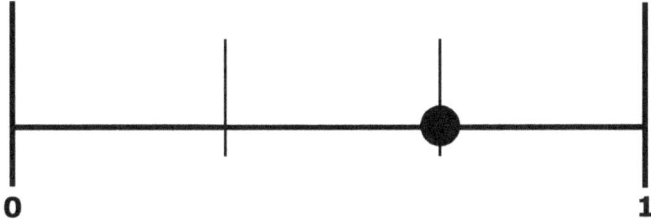

   A. 2
   B. 1/3
   C. 2/3
   D. 3/2

2. What fraction does the number line show?

   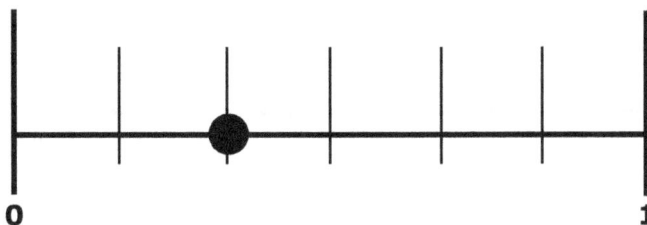

   A. 2/6
   B. 2
   C. 3/7
   D. 6/2

3. Label the fraction 5/8 where it belongs on the number line. Draw a point to show the fraction.

   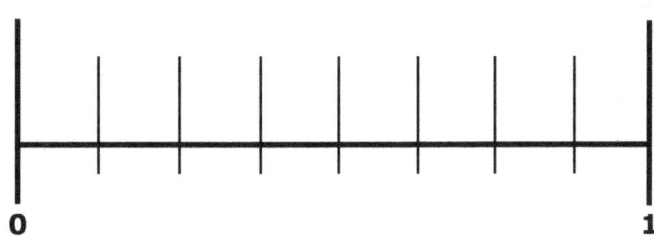

4. What fraction does the number line show? Choose the **TWO** answers that apply.

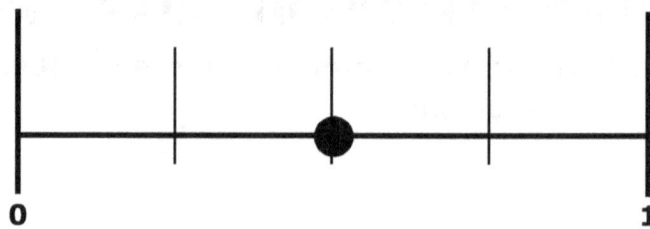

☐ ¹/₂

☐ ²/₁

☐ ²/₄

☐ ³/₆

5. How many thirds are in one whole?

   A. 3
   B. 1
   C. 0
   D. 6

6. Divide the number line into sixths.

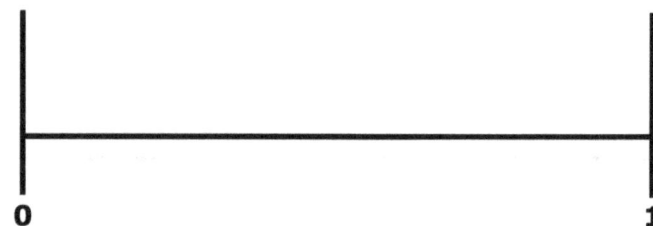

Label where the fraction ⁵/₆ belongs on the number line above. Draw a point to show the fraction.

7. What fraction does NOT belong on the number line below?

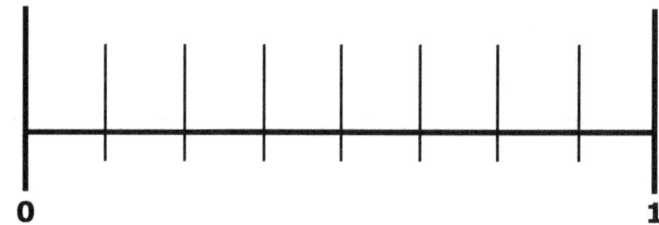

   A. ¹/₂
   B. ⁸/₈
   C. ²/₄
   D. ¹/₃

8. Which number lines could be used to find the fraction $1/3$? Choose **ALL** answers that apply.

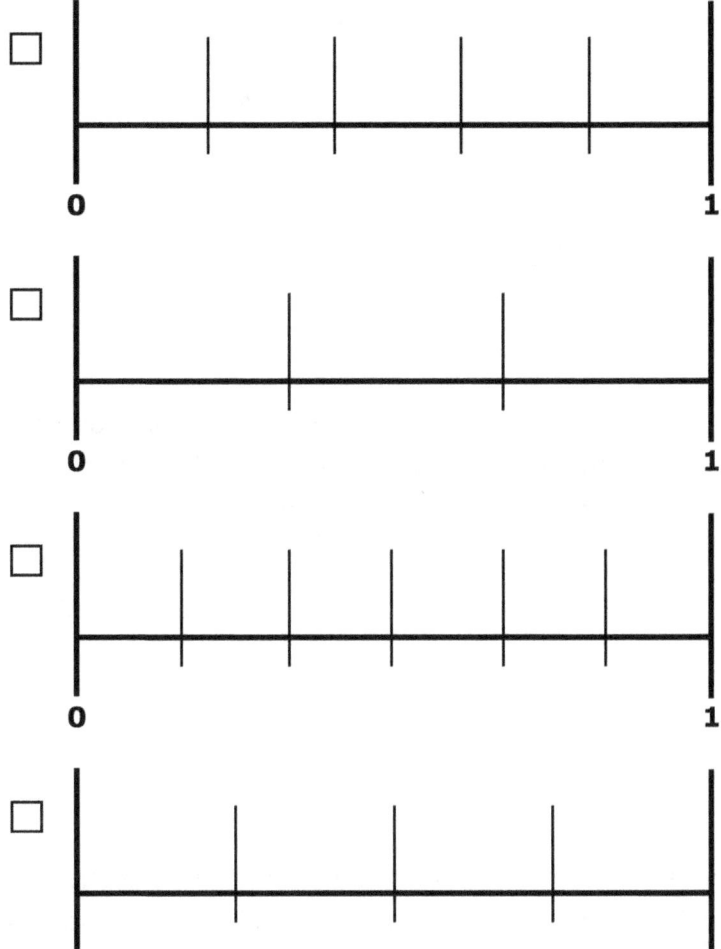

9. How far is a point at $1/4$ from $3/4$?

   A. 2
   B. $1/4$
   C. 3
   D. $2/4$

Make a number line diagram to show and explain your answer from above.

NUMBER & OPERATIONS – FRACTIONS

10. What fraction does the number line show? Choose the **TWO** answers that apply.

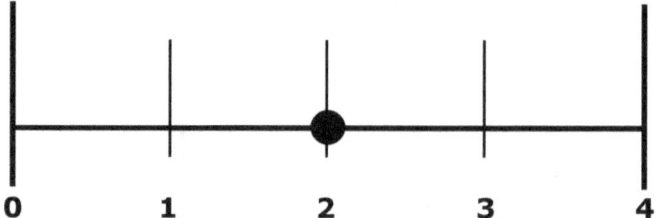

☐ $2/1$
☐ $2/4$
☐ $4/2$
☐ $0/2$

Darnell says that the fraction $4/2$ doesn't fit on the number line above because the numerator is bigger than the denominator and fractions are always less than one. Do you agree with Darnell? Why or why not? Explain your thinking below.

_____

_____

_____

11. A carpenter is making a new shelf. Each piece of wood is segmented into eighths, and he needs to cut $12/8$ of a piece of wood. How many pieces of wood will the carpenter need?

A. 12
B. 8
C. 1
D. 2

Using number lines, draw a picture to show and explain your answer to the question above.

_____

_____

_____

12. Look at how each of the number lines below is partitioned. Place each fraction on the appropriate number line. Some fractions will fit on more than one number line.

$\frac{1}{3}$ $\frac{4}{6}$ $\frac{6}{6}$ $\frac{2}{3}$ $\frac{6}{2}$

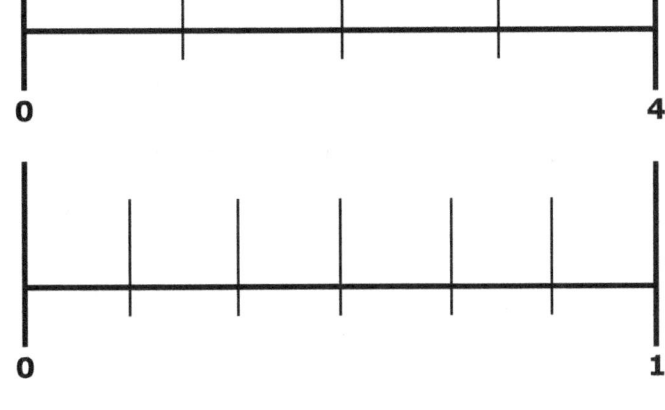

Choose a fraction that is labeled on more than one number line. Explain why this is possible.

___

NUMBER & OPERATIONS – FRACTIONS

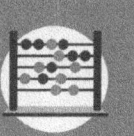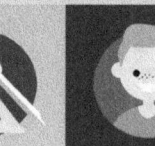

COMPARE FRACTIONS

3.NF.1.3. Compare two fractions with the same numerator or the same denominator by reasoning about their size. Recognize that comparisons are valid only when the two fractions refer to the same whole. Record the results of comparisons with the symbols >, =, < and justify the conclusions, e.g., by using a visual fraction model.

1. Choose the fraction that makes the following comparison true.

   $$\frac{2}{8} < \frac{\square}{\square}$$

   A. $\frac{1}{8}$
   B. $\frac{2}{8}$
   C. $\frac{5}{8}$
   D. $\frac{0}{8}$

2. Choose the fraction that makes the following comparison true.

   $$\frac{1}{4} < \frac{\square}{\square}$$

   A. $\frac{1}{2}$
   B. $\frac{1}{6}$
   C. $\frac{1}{5}$
   D. $\frac{1}{4}$

3. Choose the fraction that makes the following comparison true.

   $$\frac{6}{6} = \frac{\square}{\square}$$

   A. $\frac{6}{1}$
   B. $\frac{1}{1}$
   C. $\frac{1}{6}$
   D. 6

4. Which of the following fractions would fall between 0 and 1 on a number line?
   Choose **ALL** answers that apply.

   ☐ $\frac{3}{1}$
   ☐ $\frac{1}{2}$
   ☐ $\frac{1}{9}$
   ☐ $\frac{2}{1}$
   ☐ $\frac{3}{4}$

NUMBER & OPERATIONS – FRACTIONS

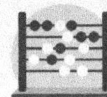

5. Choose the fraction that represents one whole.

   A. $^5/_5$

   B. $^5/_1$

   C. $^2/_1$

   D. $^{10}/_1$

   Prove how you know that the fraction you chose represents one whole. Use pictures, numbers, or words.

   _____
   _____
   _____
   _____

6. Miranda and Valentina both had ice cream sundaes for dessert. Miranda said, "I had a large ice cream sundae and I ate 2/4 of it." Valentina replied, "I ate more than you! I had a large ice cream sundae too, but I ate 4/8 of mine." Their friend Hillary said, "Valentina, you didn't eat more ice cream than Miranda. You ate the same amount."

   Who is correct? Valentina or Hillary?

   Answer: _____

   Use pictures and words to explain your thinking.

   _____
   _____
   _____
   _____

NUMBER & OPERATIONS – FRACTIONS

Use the number line below to answer the following questions.

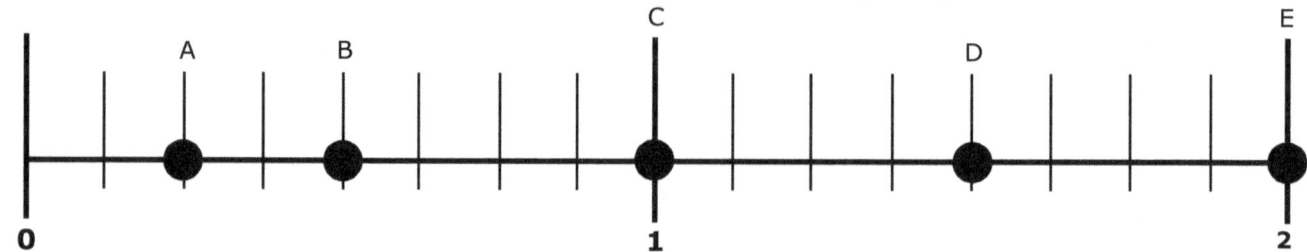

7. Which point on the number line above shows the location of the fraction 2/2 ?
   A. A
   B. B
   C. C
   D. E

8. Which fractions does letter B represent on the number line above? Choose **ALL** answers that apply.
   ☐ 2/4
   ☐ 4/4
   ☐ 1/2
   ☐ 4/1
   ☐ 4/8

9. Elijah ate 1/2 of a cheese pizza for dinner last night. Wally ate 1/4 of a pepperoni pizza for dinner last night. Wally ate more pizza than Elijah. How is this possible? Explain your thinking using pictures and words.

_____
_____
_____
_____
_____

10. Which of the following sets has the fractions listed in order from least to greatest? Choose **ALL** answers that apply.

    ☐ $\frac{1}{2}, \frac{1}{3}, \frac{1}{4}, \frac{1}{5}$

    ☐ $\frac{1}{4}, \frac{1}{3}, \frac{1}{2}, \frac{1}{1}$

    ☐ $\frac{5}{1}, \frac{4}{1}, \frac{3}{1}, \frac{2}{1}$

    ☐ $\frac{1}{1}, \frac{2}{2}, \frac{3}{3}, \frac{4}{4}$

    ☐ $\frac{1}{4}, \frac{1}{2}, \frac{3}{4}, \frac{4}{4}$

11. Place each fraction on the number lines below.

    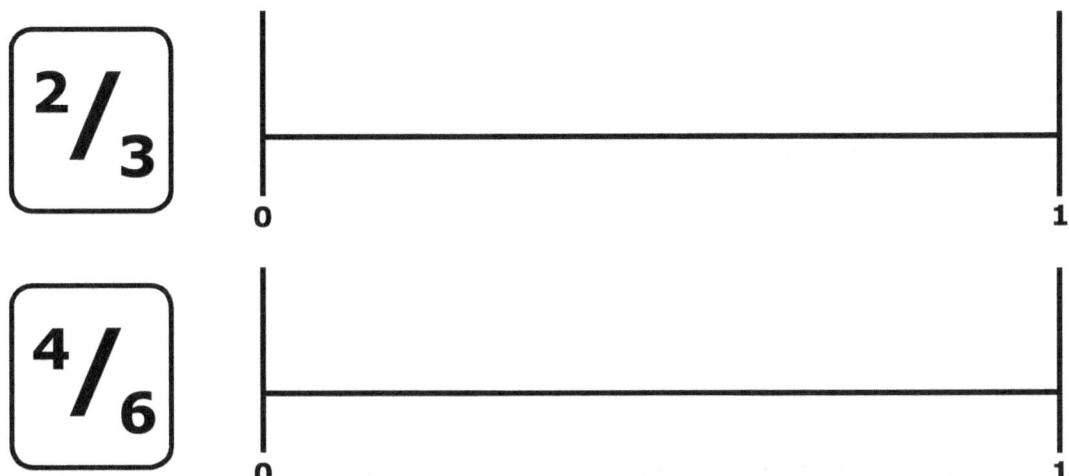

    Are these fractions equivalent? Explain how you know.

    _____

    _____

    _____

    _____

12. Mrs. Clark and Mrs. Shelton each baked an apple pie. Both pies were the same size. Mrs. Clark cut her pie into 4 slices and Mrs. Shelton cut her pie into 12 slices. Abbey ate 1 slice from Mrs. Clark's pie and Jessica ate 2 slices from Mrs. Shelton's pie. Who ate more pie? Jessica or Abbey?

    Answer: _____

NUMBER & OPERATIONS – FRACTIONS

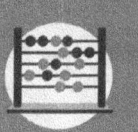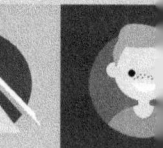

Explain how you know who ate more pie.

_____

_____

_____

_____

_____

How much pie would both girls have to eat in order to eat the same amount?

    A. Abbey: $1/4$, Jessica: $1/12$

    B. Abbey: $3/4$, Jessica: $11/12$

    C. Abbey: $4/1$, Jessica: $12/1$

    D. Abbey: $1/4$, Jessica: $3/12$

Explain how the answer you chose proves that Abbey and Jessica eat an equal amount of pie.

_____

_____

_____

_____

_____

NUMBER & OPERATIONS – FRACTIONS

MEASUREMENT AND DATA

 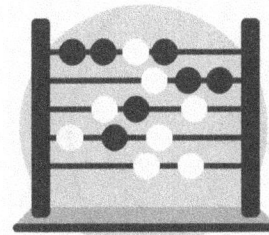 

TELL TIME & SOLVE WORD PROBLEMS INVOLVING TIME INTERVALS

3.MD.1.1. Tell and write time to the nearest minute and measure time intervals in minutes. Solve word problems involving addition and subtraction of time intervals in minutes, e.g., by representing the problem on a number line diagram.

1. What time does this clock show?

   A. 7:03
   B. 3:07
   C. 3:37
   D. 4:37

2. What time does this clock show?

   A. 10:29
   B. 6:10
   C. 11:30
   D. 6:11

 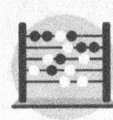        

3. How many minutes have passed between 6:30 and 7.00?

Choose **ALL** answers that apply.

☐ 30 minutes
☐ 40 minutes
☐ one hour
☐ 1 and a 1/2 hours
☐ a half hour

4. What time is shown on the number line?

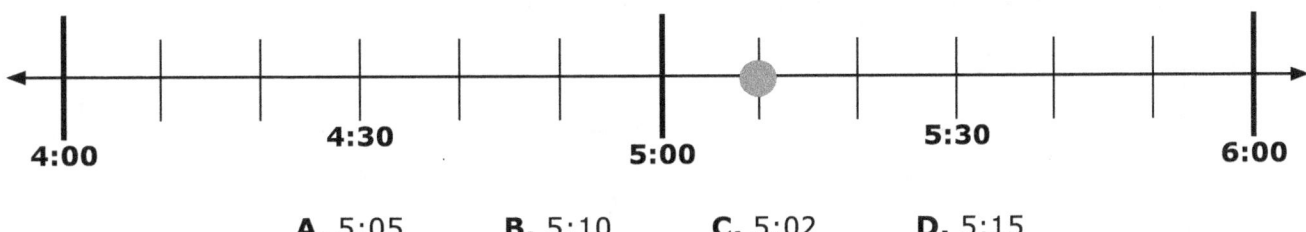

A. 5:05   **B.** 5:10   **C.** 5:02   **D.** 5:15

5. What time does this clock show?

A. 1:15
B. 3:05
C. 1:03
D. 3:07

MEASUREMENT AND DATA

6. Using your answer from above, what time will it be in 8 minutes? Draw and write the time below.

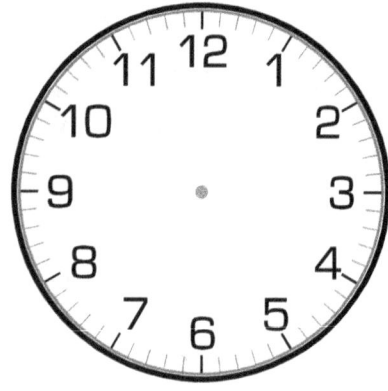
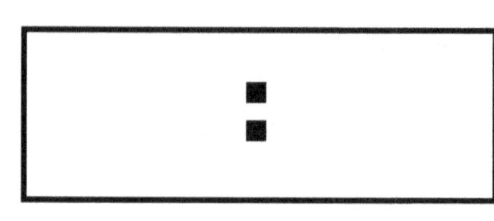

7. Chris started his chores at 7:15. It took him 35 minutes to do his chores. Which number line shows the time that Chris finished his chores?

A.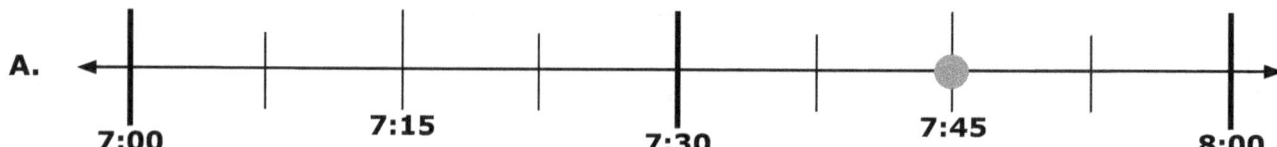

B.

C.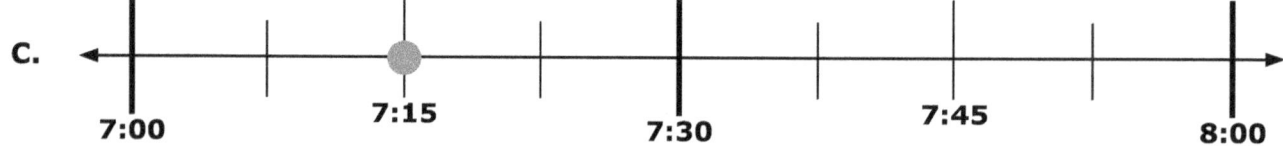

D.

 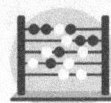        

8. How much time has passed from Clock A to Clock B? Choose **ALL** answers that apply.

Clock A   Clock B

☐ 1 hour 33 minutes
☐ 33 minutes
☐ 93 minutes
☐ 27 minutes
☐ 1 hour 27 minutes

9. Chad wants to go to the movies. He can see a movie that is 1 hour and 15 minutes long. His choices are in the table below.

Movie	Start Time	End Time
Fish and Sharks and Whales, Oh My!	2:05 p.m.	3:30 p.m.
Elementary School Musical	1:10 p.m.	2:45 p.m.
Little Lego Monsters	3:05 p.m.	4:15 p.m.

What movie has the longest showtime?

Answer: _____

What movie is Chad able to see?

Answer: _____

MEASUREMENT AND DATA

10. Betty wakes up at 6:15. It takes her 10 minutes to shower, 5 minutes to get dressed, 15 minutes to eat breakfast, and 7 minutes to gather her school materials. How long does it take Betty to get ready for school?
    - **A.** 10 minutes
    - **B.** 17 minutes
    - **C.** 30 minutes
    - **D.** 37 minutes

    What time will Betty be ready for school?
    - **A.** 6:52
    - **B.** 6:45
    - **C.** 7:00
    - **D.** 6:30

11. Zack made a number line to show the times he started playing his video game and finished playing his video game.

    Zack played his video game for 40 minutes. Which number line shows 7:15 p.m. in the correct place on Zack's number line?

    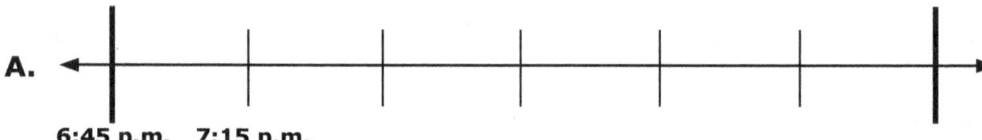

    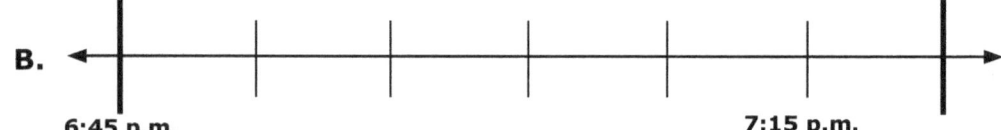

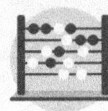

12. Oliver went to bed at 8:00 p.m. when he was finished with his evening chores. He did his homework for 35 minutes, showered for 13 minutes, made his lunch for 6 minutes, and folded laundry for 12 minutes. What time did Oliver start his evening chores?

    A. 7:00 p.m.

    B. 6:54 p.m.

    C. 7:54 p.m.

    D. 6:00 p.m.

Before Oliver started his evening chores, he ate dinner. Dinner lasted 24 minutes. What time did dinner start?

Answer: _____

       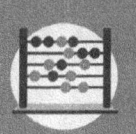  

ESTIMATE & MEASURE LIQUID VOLUME & MASS

MD.1.2. Measure and estimate liquid volumes and masses of objects using standard units of grams (g), kilograms (kg), and liters (l). Add, subtract, multiply, or divide to solve one-step word problems involving masses or volumes that are given in the same units, e.g., by using drawings to represent the problem.

1. Circle the best estimate for the mass of a pencil.

    A. 5 grams
    B. 100 grams
    C. 1 kilogram
    D. 10 kilograms

2. Circle the best estimate for the capacity of a pitcher of water?

    A. 10 liters
    B. 2 milliliters
    C. 2 liters
    D. 10 milliliters

3. Estimate the mass of each object by determining if the mass is more or less than a kilogram. Fill in the table below.

Object	Estimate: more or less than a kilogram?
cell phone	
paper airplane	
grand piano	

76   MEASUREMENT AND DATA

4. Irene is making toast in the toaster. What is the approximate mass of the toaster?
   A. 1 liter
   B. 5 liters
   C. 1 kilogram
   D. 5 grams

5. Alex is selling lemonade. About how much lemonade can fit in one pitcher of lemonade?
   A. 20 liters
   B. 2 liters
   C. 4 grams
   D. 40 kilograms

6. Which items in the kitchen are most likely to have a mass of 1 kilogram? Check **ALL** that apply.
   ☐ a bunch of bananas
   ☐ a refrigerator
   ☐ a dishwasher
   ☐ a pineapple
   ☐ an oven

7. Steve is baking a cake and is measuring the ingredients. He needs 2 liters of milk and 1 liter of cream. Shade in each container below to show the correct measurement.

Milk   Cream

How much more milk than cream does Steve need? _____

How much milk and cream does Steve need altogether? _____

Steve wants to double his recipe to make 2 cakes.
How much milk and cream will Steve need altogether now? _____

MEASUREMENT AND DATA

       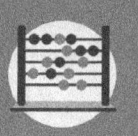  

8. Nyasia is filling her fish tank with water. She is using a 4 liter bucket to add water to the tank. The tank needs 28 liters of water in order to be full. How many times does Nyasia need to fill the 4 liter bucket with water and add it to the tank until it is full?
    A. 4 times
    B. 5 times
    C. 6 times
    D. 7 times

9. Harper is traveling and wants to know how much her luggage is going to cost at the airport. She has 2 pieces of luggage. 1 luggage has a mass of 25 kilograms and the second luggage has a mass of 15 kilograms.

    What is the total mass of Harper's luggage?

    Answer: _____

    The fee for luggage is free for the first 15 kilograms and $5 each for each kilogram over 15 kilograms. How much will Harper have to pay for her luggage? Show your work using pictures, numbers, or words.

    Answer: _____

10. A weightlifter wants to lift a bar that has a mass of 75 kilograms. Right now, the bar has a 10 kilogram weight, a 5 kilogram weight, and a 2 ½ kilogram weight on each end of the bar. How much more mass does the weightlifter need to add to the bar so that it will have a total mass of 75 kilograms?
    A. 17 ½ kilograms
    B. 35 kilograms
    C. 40 kilograms
    D. 35 ½ kilograms

MEASUREMENT AND DATA

11. Mom prepared a total of 6 liters of hot chocolate. The glasses of hot chocolate she prepared are shown below.
    How much hot chocolate is in each glass?
    - **A.** 24 liters
    - **B.** 1 ½ liters
    - **C.** 4 liters
    - **D.** 1 ¼ liter

12. Dan has 325 mL of water in a container. He wants to pour the water into smaller beakers. Each beaker can hold 50 mL of water. How many beakers will Dan need?
    - **A.** 5 beakers
    - **B.** 6 beakers
    - **C.** 7 beakers
    - **D.** 8 beakers

    How many more mL of water could Dan fit into the last beaker?
    - **A.** 325 mL
    - **B.** 25 mL
    - **C.** 300 mL
    - **D.** 0 mL

       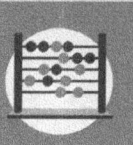  

DRAW SCALED PICTURE & BAR GRAPHS & SOLVE PROBLEMS

3.MD.2.3. Draw a scaled picture graph and a scaled bar graph to represent a data set with several categories. Solve one- and two-step "how many more" and "how many less" problems using information presented in scaled bar graphs. For example, draw a bar graph in which each square in the bar graph might represent 5 pets.

1. Mrs. Hussain's class voted on their favorite school subjects. The choices were: Reading, Writing, Math, and Science. The tally table below was used to record the votes.

Subject	Number of Votes
Reading	|||| ||||
Writing	||||
Math	|||| ||
Science	|||

How many students voted for Reading as their favorite subject?
A. 8
B. 9
C. 2
D. 3

What subject got the least number of votes?
A. Reading
B. Writing
C. Math
D. Science

80 MEASUREMENT AND DATA

2. Luis created a pictograph to show the different kinds of animals he observed on a nature walk. The graph shows the animals he saw and how many of each type.

Type of Animal	Number of Animals
Squirrel	 🐾 🐾 🐾
Deer	 🐾
Blue Jay	 🐾 🐾 🐾 🐾
Chipmunk	 🐾 🐾

Each 🐾 represents 2 animals.

How many Blue Jays and Chipmunks did Luis see?
A. 12
B. 6
C. 8
D. 5

How many Deer did Luis see?
A. 2
B. 0
C. 3
D. 1

3. The Third Grade Class had a bake sale to raise money for their class trip. They made brownies, chocolate chip cookies, cupcakes, and fudge. The pictograph below shows how many of each dessert they sold.

Type of Dessert	Number Sold
Brownies	 🍪🍪🍪🍪🍪
Chocolate Chip Cookies	 🍪🍪🍪🍪🍪🍪🍪
Cupcakes	 🍪🍪🍪🍪🍪
Fudge	 🍪🍪🍪

Each 🍪 represents 4 desserts.

How many more cupcakes than fudge did they sell?
A. 2
B. 5
C. 3
D. 8

How many chocolate chip cookies did they sell?
A. 6
B. 28
C. 7
D. 26

4. Raquel created a bar graph to show the items collected for the school's clothing drive. The bar graph below shows the types of items collected and how many of each type.

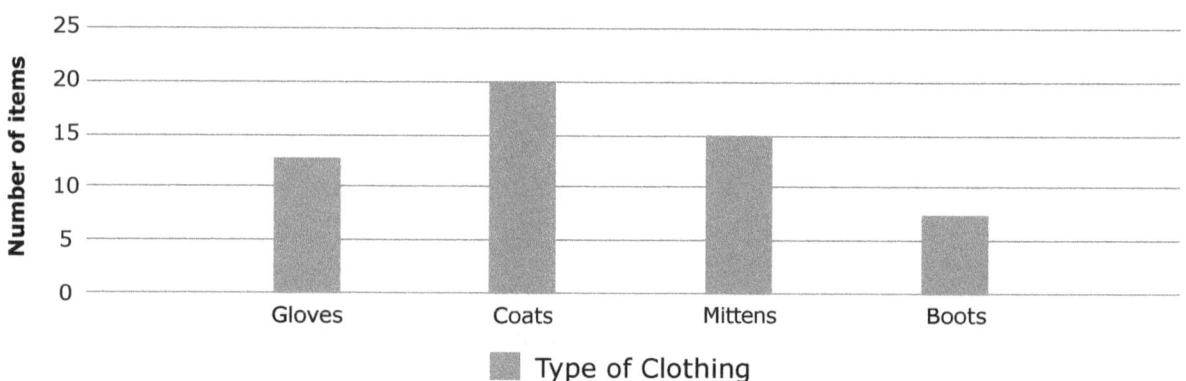

How many coats and mittens did the school collect?
A. 7
B. 35
C. 14
D. 40

How many boots did the school collect?
A. 5
B. 10
C. 4
D. 7

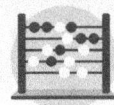

5. Cam wanted to create a bar graph to show how many pages he read last week. The bar graph below shows how many pages Cam read on Monday, Tuesday, Wednesday, and Thursday.

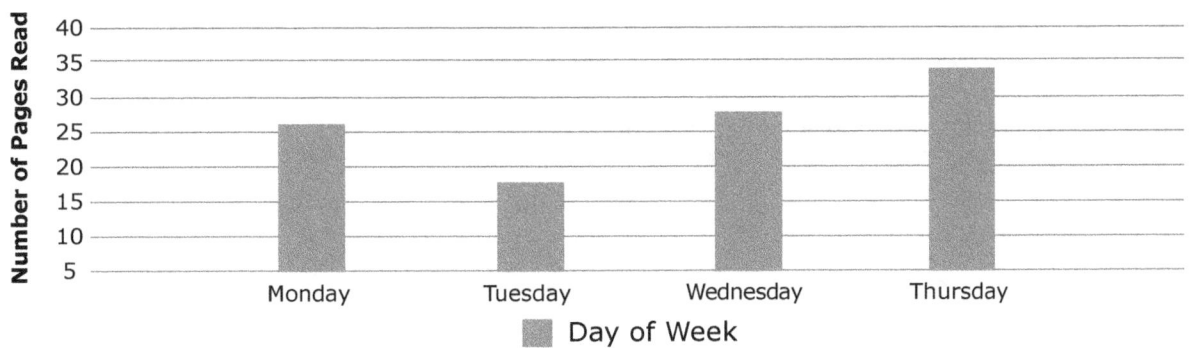

On what day of the week did Cam read the most pages?
A. Monday
B. Tuesday
C. Wednesday
D. Thursday

How many more pages did Cam read on Monday than Tuesday?
A. 8
B. 2
C. 10
D. 12

6. The students in Ms. Horn's first grade class voted for their favorite farm animals. The bar graph below shows how the students the voted.

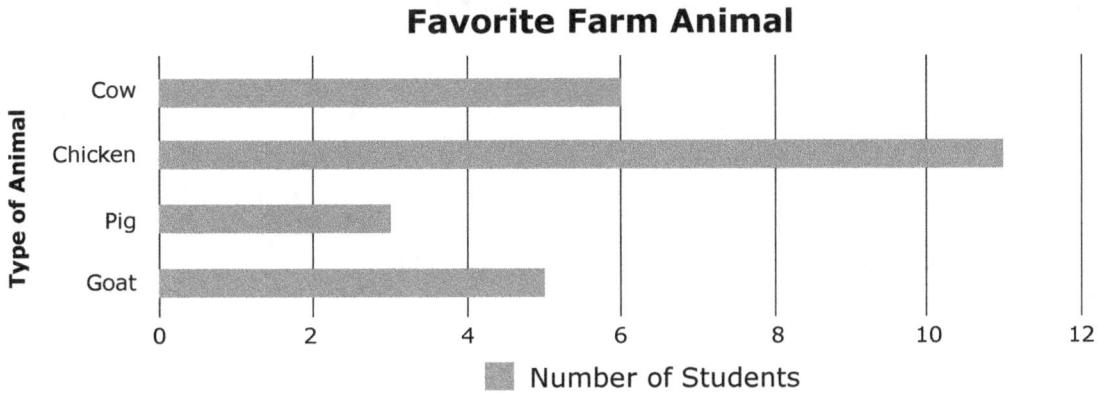

MEASUREMENT AND DATA

What farm animal was the least popular?
A. Goat
B. Pig
C. Chicken
D. Cow

How many more students voted for chickens than goats?
A. 4
B. 5
C. 6
D. 7

7. Matilda is taking a poll of her classmates' favorite fruits. 2 students voted for pears. 4 students voted for bananas. 6 students voted for oranges. 12 students voted for apples.

Complete the pictograph below to show the results of her poll.

Favorite Fruit	Number of Students
Apple	🍎 🍎 🍎 🍎 🍎 🍎
Orange	
Banana	
Pear	

Each 🍎 = 2 votes.

How many more students voted for oranges than pears?
A. 4
B. 3
C. 2
D. 1

How many students voted for bananas and pears?
A. 4
B. 5
C. 6
D. 7

8. The school store sold many items last week. The store sold 35 erasers, 40 smelly pencils, 15 pencil sharpeners, and 12 pens.

   Complete the bar graph below to show the number of items the school store sold last week. Each square should represent 5 items.

   Number of Items Sold

   _____ _____ _____ _____

   Items Sold

   What **TWO** items were the most popular?
   ☐ erasers
   ☐ smelly pencils
   ☐ pencil sharpeners
   ☐ pens

   How many items were sold altogether?

   Answer: _____

9. This graph shows the number of books in the classroom libraries of four different classrooms.

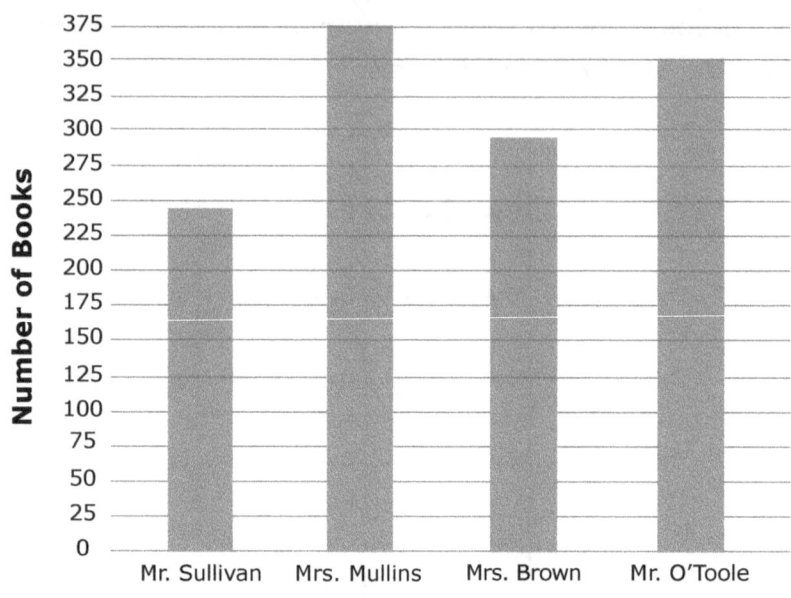

Which teachers have between 300 and 400 books in their classroom libraries?
- [ ] Mr. Sullivan
- [ ] Mrs. Mullins
- [ ] Mrs. Brown
- [ ] Mr. O'Toole

Sharon's teacher has 350 books in her classroom library. Carolyn's teacher has about 100 less books than Sharon's teacher. Who is Carolyn's teacher?
- A. Mr. Sullivan
- B. Mrs. Mullins
- C. Mrs. Brown
- D. Mr. O'Toole

Which teachers have between 900 and 1,000 books in their classroom libraries altogether? Choose **ALL** answers that apply.
- [ ] Mrs. Mullins, Mrs. Brown, Mr. O'Toole
- [ ] Mrs. Mullins, Mr. O'Toole
- [ ] Mr. Sullivan, Mrs. Brown, Mr. O'Toole
- [ ] Mr. Sullivan, Mrs. Mullins, Mr. O'Toole

10. Washington Elementary School is collecting data about students' favorite sports. The table below shows the data that was collected.

Favorite Sport	Number of Students
Soccer	79
Football	110
Baseball	95
Tennis	60

Use the information from the table to create a bar graph. Start your scale at 50. Each square should represent 10 students.

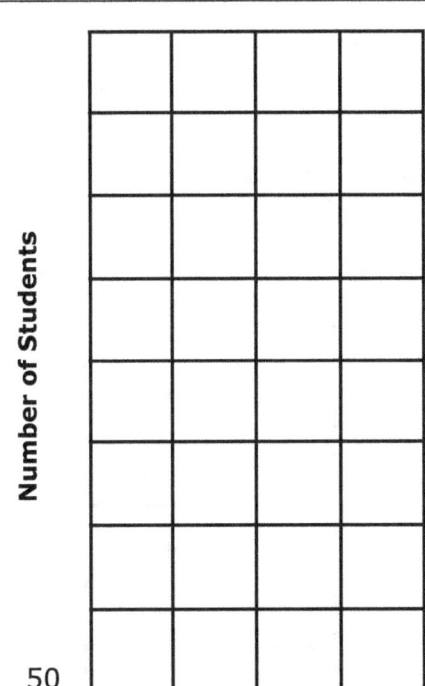

Favorite Sport

How many more students voted for football than tennis?
   A. 30
   B. 40
   C. 50
   D. 60

Choose the sequence that shows the students' favorite sports in order from least favorite to most favorite.

    A. soccer, football, baseball, tennis
    B. football, baseball, soccer, tennis
    C. tennis, soccer, baseball, football
    D. tennis, soccer, football, baseball

How many students voted altogether?

Answer: _____

Explain how you know how many students voted altogether.

_____

_____

11. A group of friends collect sports cards. Kim has 140 sports cards. James has 20 less sports cards than Kim. Mark has 30 more cards than James. Dawn has twice as many sports cards as James. *Complete the bar graph to show how many sports cards each friend has.* Start your scale at 100. Each square should represent 20 sports cards.

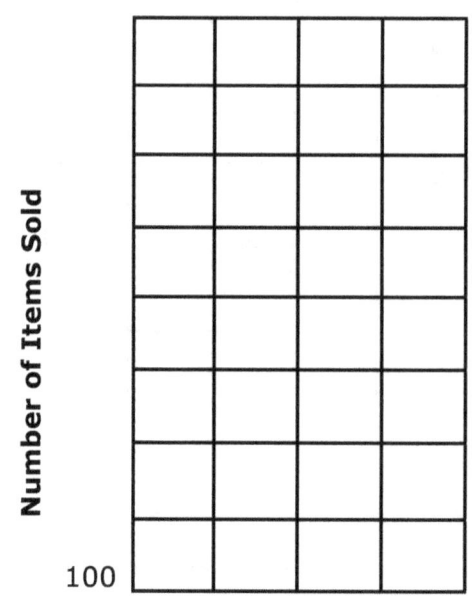

Name of Friends

88   MEASUREMENT AND DATA

Choose the sequence that shows the amount of sports cards each friend has in order from greatest to least.

A. Dawn, Kim, Mark, James
B. James, Kim, Mark, Dawn
C. Kim, James, Mark, Dawn
D. Dawn, Mark, Kim, James

12. The Third Grade Class went on a field trip to explore how insects adapt to survive in their natural habitat. They netted various insects in a large open field. They caught 25 pill bugs. They caught twice as many spiders as pill bugs. They caught 25 more ants than spiders, and they caught 15 less ladybugs than pill bugs.

Complete the pictograph to show the types of insects the Third Grade Class caught and how many of each type they caught.

Type of Insect	Number of Insects
Pill bug	
Spider	
Ant	
Ladybug	

Each 🐜 represents 10 insects.

How many spiders and ants did The Third Grade Class catch?

A. 50
B. 75
C. 100
D. 125

Write the insects that The Third Grade Class caught in order from least to greatest.

_____, _____, _____, _____

How many insects did the Third Grade Class collect altogether? Choose **ALL** answers that apply.

☐ Greater than 100
☐ 160
☐ Greater than 200
☐ Less than 100
☐ 150
☐ Greater than 150

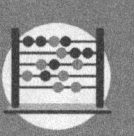

MEASURE LENGTHS & CREATE LINE PLOTS

3.MD.2.4. Generate measurement data by measuring lengths using rulers marked with halves and fourths of an inch. Show the data by making a line plot, where the horizontal scale is marked off in appropriate units – whole numbers, halves, or quarters.

1. What is the length of the envelope?

   Each unit represents 1 inch

   A. 1 inch
   B. 2 inches
   C. 3 inches
   D. 4 inches

2. What is the length of the video game controller in centimeters?

   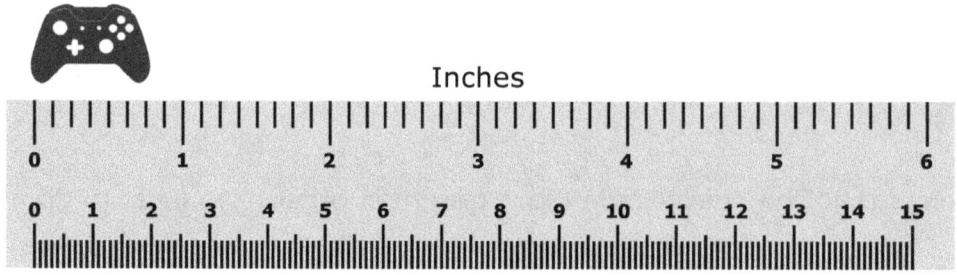

   A. 1 centimeter
   B. 2 centimeters
   C. 3 centimeters
   D. 4 centimeters

3. What is the length of the slice of pizza to the nearest 1/2 inch?

Each unit represents 1 inch

- A. 1 inch
- B. 1 1/2 inches
- C. 2 inches
- D. 2 1/2 inches

4. About how long is a paper clip?
   - A. 4 miles
   - B. 4 feet
   - C. 4 centimeters
   - D. 4 millimeters

5. Which of these could be used to measure the length of a football field? Choose **ALL** answers that apply.
   - ☐ Feet
   - ☐ Inches
   - ☐ Miles
   - ☐ Yards
   - ☐ Kilometers
   - ☐ Meters

6. What is the length of the scissors to the nearest quarter inch?

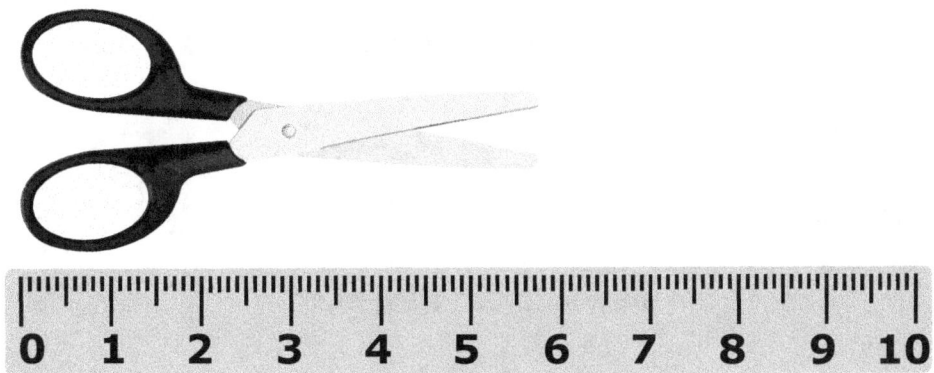

Each unit represents 1 inch

- A. 5 inches
- B. 5 1/4 inches
- C. 5 2/4 inches
- D. 5 3/4 inches

7. The lengths of some bunny hops are shown below.

Bunny Hop Lengths (feet)

How many bunnies jumped 1 foot?

A. 0
B. 1
C. 2
D. 3

What length did the bunnies hop most often?

A. 1 foot
B. 2 feet
C. 2 $\frac{1}{4}$ feet
D. 3 $\frac{1}{2}$ feet

8. How much longer is the paintbrush than the pencil?

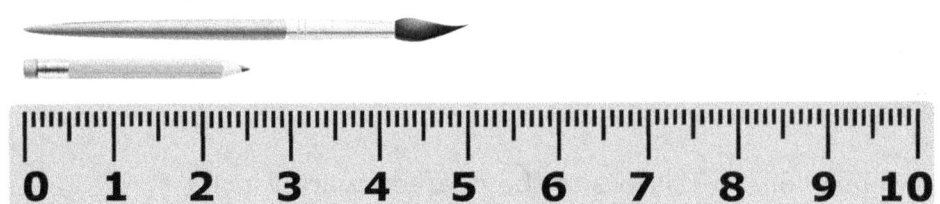

Each unit represents 1 inch

A. 5 inches
B. 2 $\frac{1}{2}$ inches
C. 3 inches
D. 3 $\frac{1}{2}$ inches

How long are the pencil and the paintbrush altogether?

A. 5 inches
B. 5 $\frac{1}{2}$ inches
C. 6 $\frac{1}{2}$ inches
D. 7 $\frac{1}{2}$ inches

9. The table below shows the different distances from Luke's house to different places in town.

Location	Distance from Luke's House
Library	6 km
Grocery Store	3 1/2 km
Gas Station	2 1/2 km
Park	4 km
Town Center	6 km

Create a line plot that shows all of the measurements.

10. The lengths of some friendship bracelets are shown below.

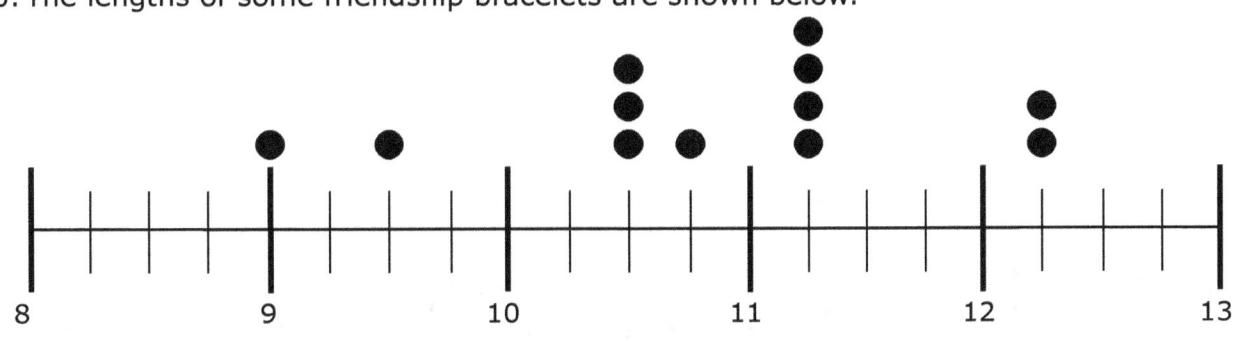

How many friendship bracelets are less than 11 inches long?
    A. 4
    B. 5
    C. 6
    D. 7

       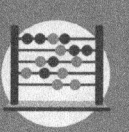  

How many more friendship bracelets were 11 $\frac{1}{4}$ inches long than 10 $\frac{1}{2}$ inches long?

A. 1
B. 2
C. 3
D. 4

11. The table below shows the distances different paper airplanes traveled.

Location	Distance from Luke's House
Paper Airplane 1	10 $\frac{1}{4}$ inches
Paper Airplane 2	7 inches
Paper Airplane 3	13 inches
Paper Airplane 4	12 $\frac{3}{4}$ inches
Paper Airplane 5	10 $\frac{1}{4}$ inches
Paper Airplane 6	10 $\frac{1}{4}$ inches
Paper Airplane 7	7 inches

Create a line plot that shows all the distances the paper airplanes traveled.

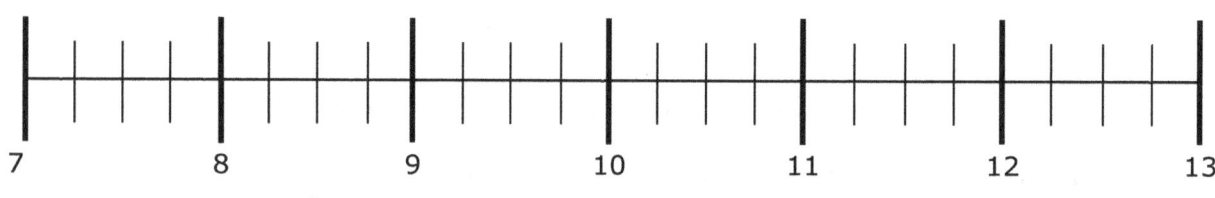

Distance Paper Airplanes Traveled (inches)

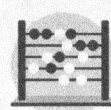

What paper airplanes traveled between 8 and 11 inches? Choose **ALL** answers that apply.

☐ Paper Airplane 1
☐ Paper Airplane 2
☐ Paper Airplane 3
☐ Paper Airplane 4
☐ Paper Airplane 5
☐ Paper Airplane 6
☐ Paper Airplane 7

How many fewer airplanes traveled a distance of 8 $\frac{1}{2}$ inches than 10 $\frac{1}{4}$ inches?

A. 1
B. 2
C. 3
D. 4

12. Andrew went fishing. The lengths of the fish he caught are shown below.

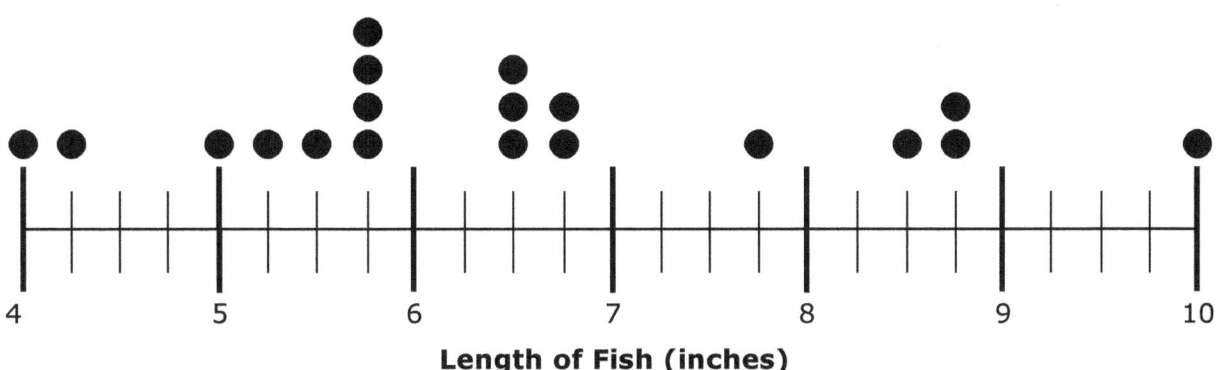

Length of Fish (inches)

How many fish did Andrew catch?

Answer: _____

Did Andrew catch more fish greater than 7 inches or less than 7 inches? Circle your answer.

Greater than 7 inches   **Less than 7 inches**

MEASUREMENT AND DATA

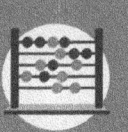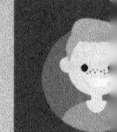

Explain how you know.

___

How many more fish measured 5 ³/₄ inches than 6 ³/₄ inches?
- **A.** 1
- **B.** 2
- **C.** 3
- **D.** 4

Which measurements had only 1 fish? Write your answer below.

___

RECOGNIZE AREA

3.MD.3.5. Recognize area as an attribute of plane figures and understand concepts of area measurement.

1. Count the square units to find the area.

   A. 12 square units
   B. 4 square units
   C. 2 square units
   D. 8 square units

2. Count the square units to find the area.

   A. 12 square units
   B. 3 square units
   C. 14 square units
   D. 4 square units

3. What is the area of the shape below?

   A. 12 square units
   B. 3 square units
   C. 6 square units
   D. 9 square units

MEASUREMENT AND DATA

4. Which of these objects would have the most square units?
   A. a chocolate bar with 8 squares
   B. a square of tiled floor
   C. a window pane with 4 panes
   D. a sheet of graph paper with 36 squares

5. Which of these objects would most likely have the greatest area?
   A. a stamp
   B. a beach towel
   C. a cell phone cover
   D. an envelope

6. Which rectangle has a greater area?

   A

   B

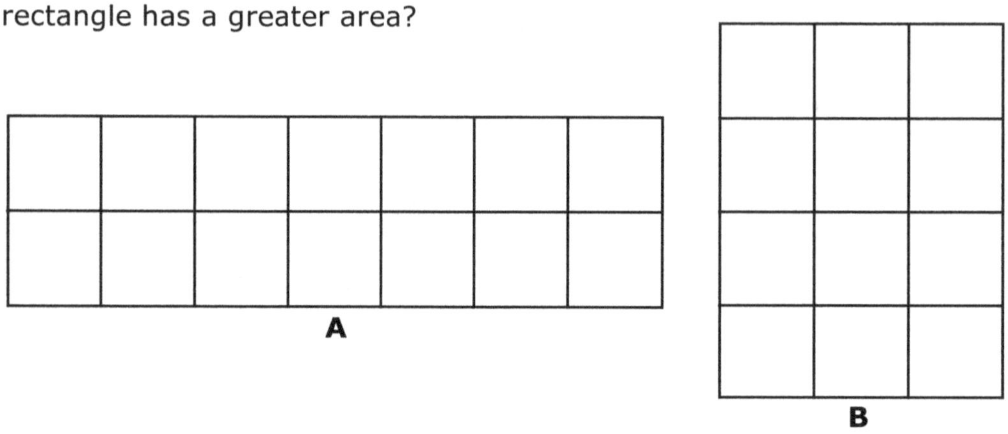

   Answer: _____

   How do you know which rectangle has a greater area?
   A. It is wider.
   B. It is longer.
   C. It has the most squares in each row.
   D. It takes up the most space.

7. Count the square units to find the area of the figure below.

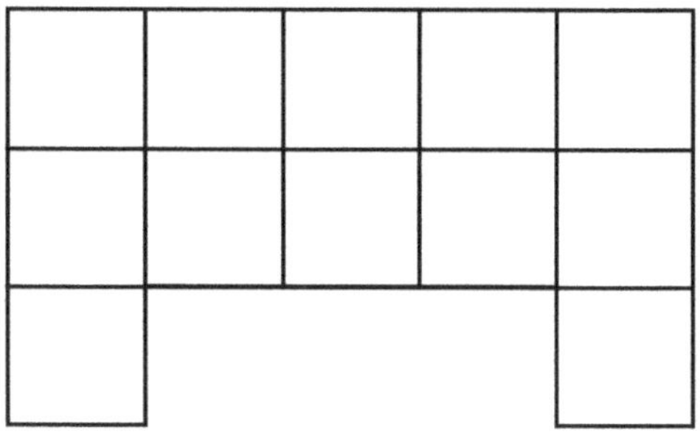

   A. 15 square units
   B. 12 square units
   C. 18 square units
   D. You cannot find the area of this figure.

MEASUREMENT AND DATA

8. Which of the following statements about these rectangles are true? Choose **ALL** answers that apply.

☐ The area of rectangle A is greater than the area of rectangle B.
☐ The areas rectangle A and B are equal.
☐ The area of rectangle B is 24 square units.
☐ The area of rectangle B is greater than the area of rectangle A.
☐ The area of rectangle A is 24 square units.
☐ Rectangle B takes up more space than rectangle A.

9. Aaron is eating a square sandwich. He says that the sandwich has an area of 18 square units. His friend Brett said that's not possible. Who do you agree with? Explain why.

_____

_____

_____

_____

_____

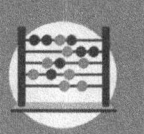

10. A rectangle has a length of 7 square units and a width of 4 square units. A square has a length of 6 square units. What shape has a greater area?

    Answer: _____

    Explain how you know which shape has a greater area.

    _____

    _____

11. A square has a length of 8 square units. A rectangle has a length of 5 square units and a width of 8 square units. How much greater is the area of the square than the rectangle?
    - **A.** 5 square units
    - **B.** 8 square units
    - **C.** 24 square units
    - **D.** The areas are the same.

    The area of the square is _____ square units.

    The area of the rectangle is _____ square units.

12. Sam wants to design a garden that has an area of 42 square units. He needs to determine how long and wide each side of the garden should be. What are the possible measurements Sam can use? Choose **ALL** answers that apply.

    Each side can be 12 square units.
    - ☐ The length can be 2 square units and the width can be 21 square units.
    - ☐ The width can be 6 square units and the length can be 7 square units.
    - ☐ The length can be 9 square units and the width can be 12 square units.
    - ☐ The length can be 14 square units and the width can be 3 square units.

    Which length and width do you think Sam should choose? Explain why.

    _____

    _____

    _____

MEASUREMENT AND DATA

MEASURE AREA

3.MD.3.6. Measure areas by counting unit squares (square cm, square m, square in, square ft, and improvised units).

1. What is the area of the shaded figure? Each square is a 1 x 1 square meter.

   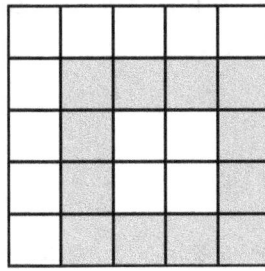

   A. 25 square meters
   B. 16 square meters
   C. 12 square meters
   D. 13 square meters

2. What is the area of the shaded figure? Each square is a 1 x 1 square centimeter.

   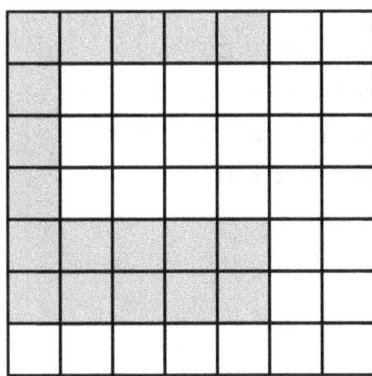

   A. 18 square centimeters
   B. 30 square centimeters
   C. 49 square centimeters
   D. 31 square centimeters

3. Find the area of the shaded figure. Each square is a 1 x 1 square inch.

   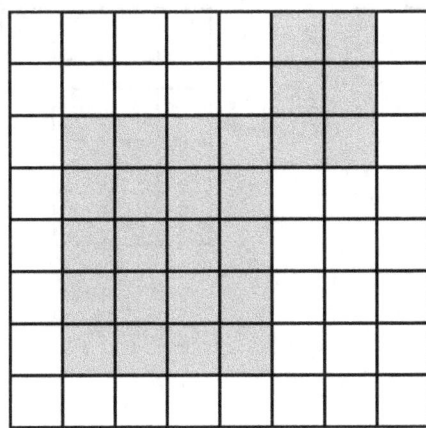

   A. 42 square inches
   B. 36 square inches
   C. 64 square inches
   D. 26 square inches

4. What is the area of the figure below? Each square is a 1 x 1 square centimeter.

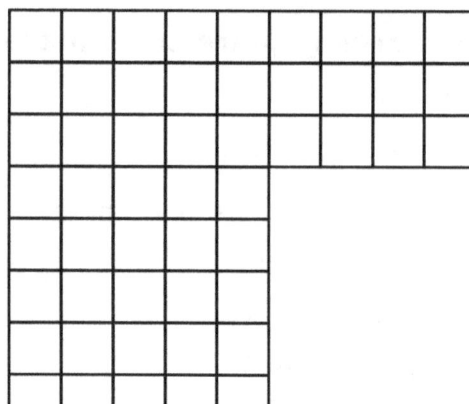

A. 72 square centimeters
B. 20 square centimeters
C. 52 square centimeters
D. 92 square centimeters

5. What is the area of the figure below? Each square is a 1 x 1 square meter.

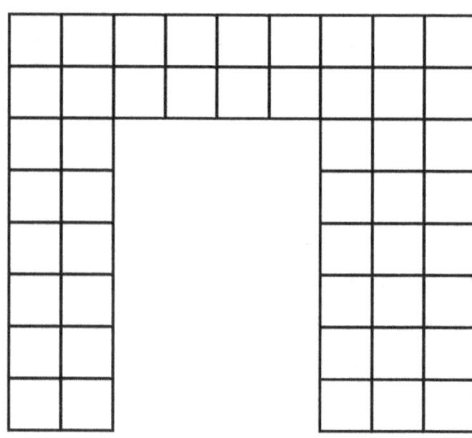

A. 48 square meters
B. 72 square meters
C. 64 square meters
D. 24 square meters

6. Which shapes have an area of 12 square inches? Choose **ALL** answers that apply.

☐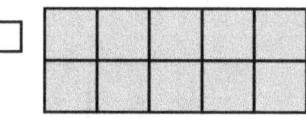

☐ (shape)

☐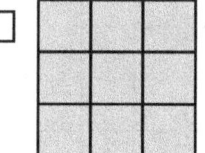

☐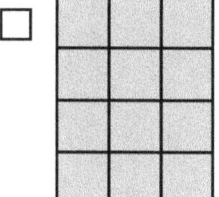

7. What is the area of the shaded figure? Each square is a 1 x 1 square inch.

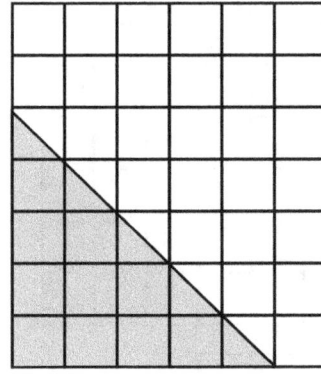

   A. 10 square inches
   B. 11 $\frac{1}{2}$ square inches
   C. 12 square inches
   D. 12 $\frac{1}{2}$ square inches

8. Draw a figure that has an area of 14 square units.

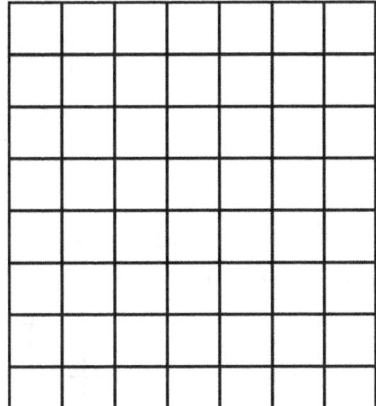

   What is the length of the figure you created? _____ square units

   What is the width of the figure you created?   _____ square units

9. What is the area of the shaded figure? Each square is a 1 x 1 square centimeter.

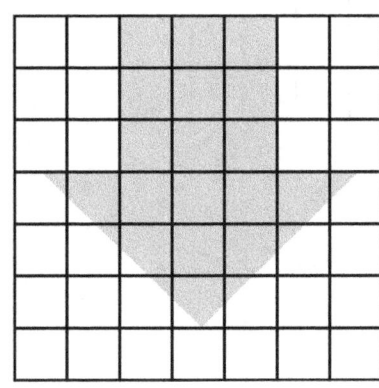

   A. 18 square centimeters
   B. 16 $\frac{1}{2}$ square centimeters
   C. 20 square centimeters
   D. 21 square centimeters

10. The Third Grade Class is making a mosaic in art class. Each student will have 18 square inches to make a design. What are some of the different ways the students can use the squares to fill up 18 square inches? Choose **ALL** answers that apply.

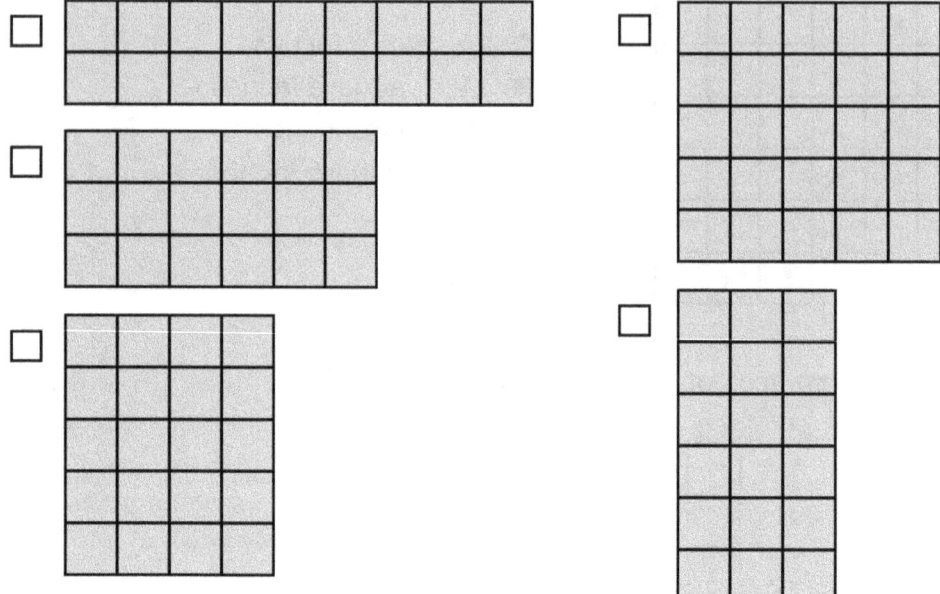

Show another way that the students can use the squares to fill up 18 square inches. This must be different than any of the above answer choices.

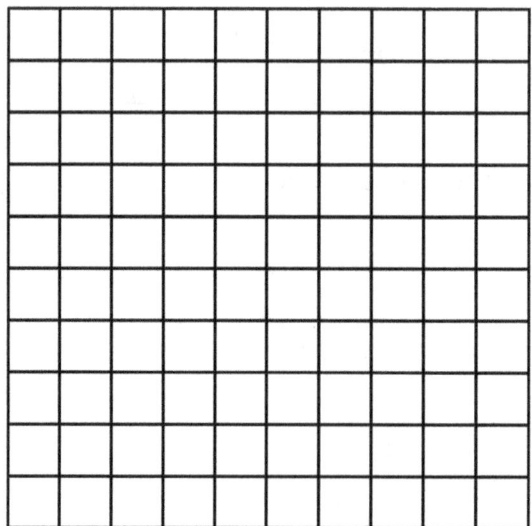

11. What is the area of the shaded figure below? Each square is a 1 x 1 square centimeter.

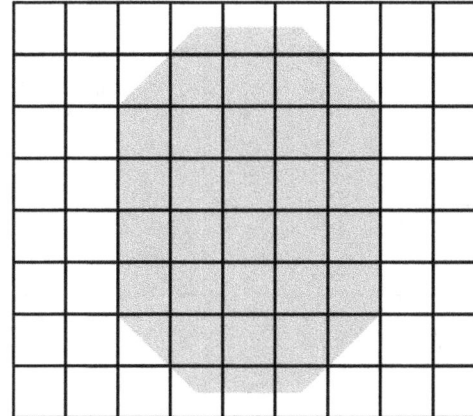

A. 28 square centimeters
B. 31 square centimeters
C. 37 square centimeters
D. 35 square centimeters

Draw a different figure that has the same area as the figure above.

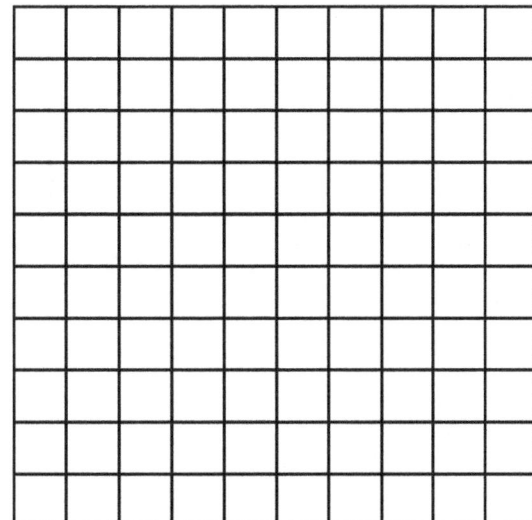

12. Cathy is building a snow wall that has a length of 12 square feet and a width of 10 square feet. Jay is building a snow wall that has an area that is 20 less square feet than Cathy's. Destiny is building a snow wall that has an area that is 30 more square feet than Cathy's.

    What are the areas of the snow walls in order from least to greatest?
    A. Cathy, Jay, Destiny
    B. Destiny, Jay, Cathy
    C. Jay, Cathy, Destiny
    D. Jay, Destiny, Cathy

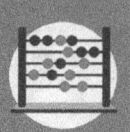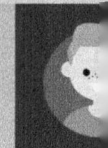

How much greater is the area of Destiny's snow wall than Jay's snow wall?

    A. 20 square feet

    B. 30 square feet

    C. 40 square feet

    D. 50 square feet

What is the area of all 3 snow walls altogether?

Answer: _____

RELATE AREA TO MULTIPLICATION AND ADDITION

3.MD.3.7. Relate area to the operations of multiplication and addition.

1. Add to find the area.

   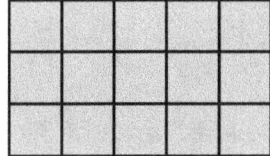

   5 squares in each row, 3 rows

   A. 3 + 3 + 3 = 9 square units
   B. 5 + 5 + 5 = 15 square units
   C. 3 + 5 + 3 + 5 = 16 square units
   D. 5 + 3 = 8 square units

2. Multiply to find the area.

   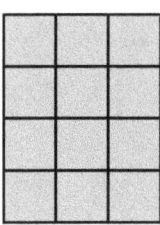

   Length: 4 square units
   Width: 3 square units

   A. 3 x 1 = 3 square units
   B. 4 x 1 = 4 square units
   C. 4 x 3 = 12 square units
   D. 4 x 3 + 4 x 3 = 24 square units

3. Which expressions could be used to find the area of the shape below? Choose **ALL** answers that apply.

   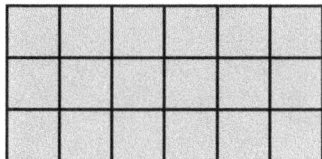

   ☐ 3 x 6
   ☐ 3 + 6 + 3 + 6
   ☐ 6 + 6 + 6
   ☐ 6 + 3
   ☐ 3 + 3 + 3 + 3 + 3 + 3

4. What is the area of the square?

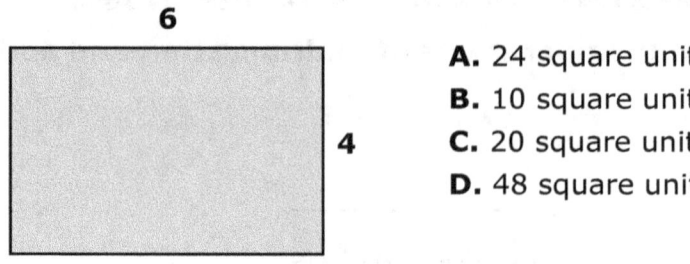

A. 24 square units
B. 10 square units
C. 20 square units
D. 48 square units

5. Which of the following rectangles have an area of 30 square units? Choose **ALL** that apply.

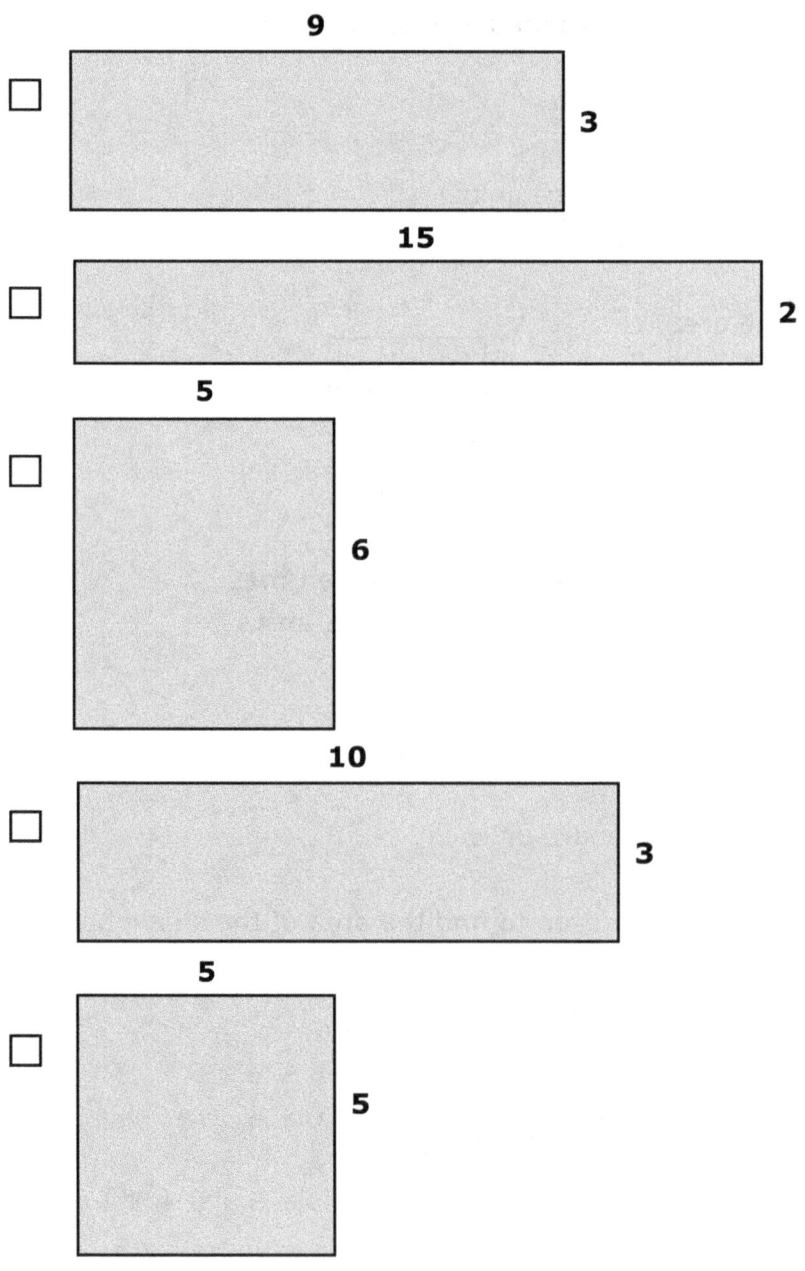

6. The basketball court has an area of 48 square yards. The length of the basketball court is 8 yards. What is the width of the basketball court?

WIDTH

8 yds.

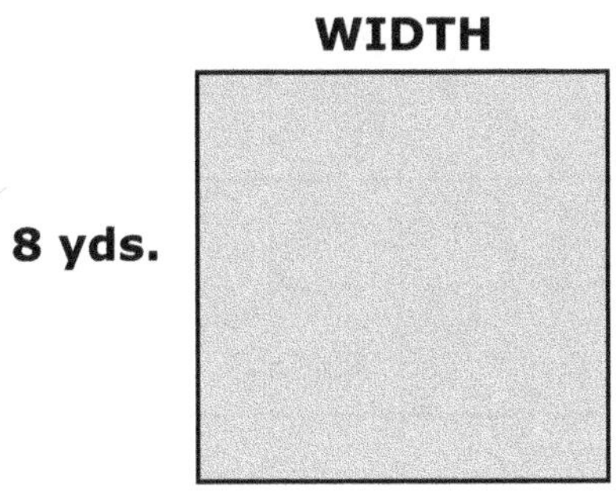

A. 40 yards
B. 8 yards
C. 6 yards
D. 32 yards

7. A garden has an area of 54 square meters. The width of the garden is 6 meters. What is the length of the garden?
   A. 9 meters
   B. 48 meters
   C. 6 meters
   D. 42 meters

8. Which expressions can be used to find the total area of the rectangle below? Choose **ALL** answers that apply.

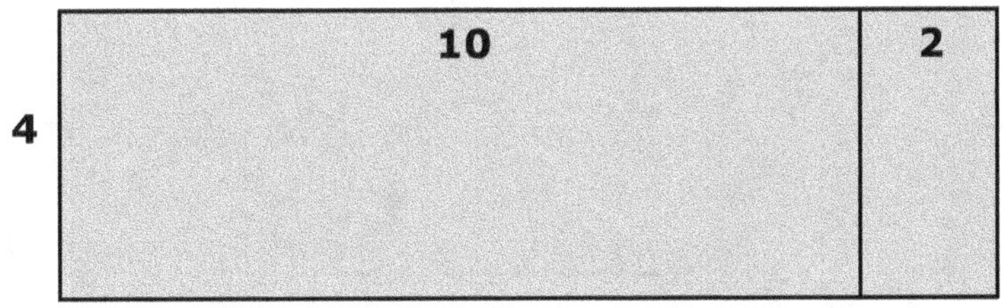

☐ 10 x 4 x 2
☐ (4 + 10) x (4 x 2)
☐ 40 + 8
☐ 4 x 12
☐ (4 x 10) + (4 x 2)

What is the total area of the rectangle above?

Answer: _____ square units

9. Which expressions can be used to find the total area of the rectangle below? Choose **ALL** answers that apply.

☐ 15 + 3 + 15 + 3
☐ (10 x 3) + (5 x 3)
☐ 15 x 3
☐ 30 + 15
☐ (10 + 3) x (5 + 3)

What is the area of the rectangle above?

Answer: _____ square units

10. Use the figure below to answer the following questions

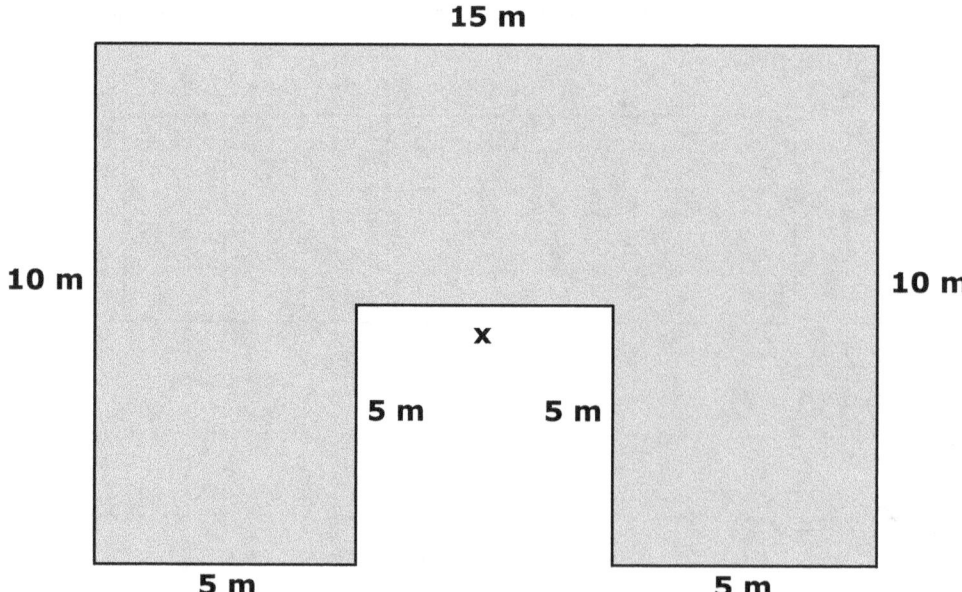

Draw lines to show how the figure could be decomposed to help find the area.

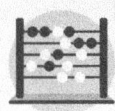

What is the value of X?
- A. 5 meters
- B. 10 meters
- C. 15 meters
- D. 20 meters

What is the total area of the shape?
- A. 50 meters
- B. 75 meters
- C. 100 meters
- D. 125 meters

11. Use the figure below to answer the following questions.

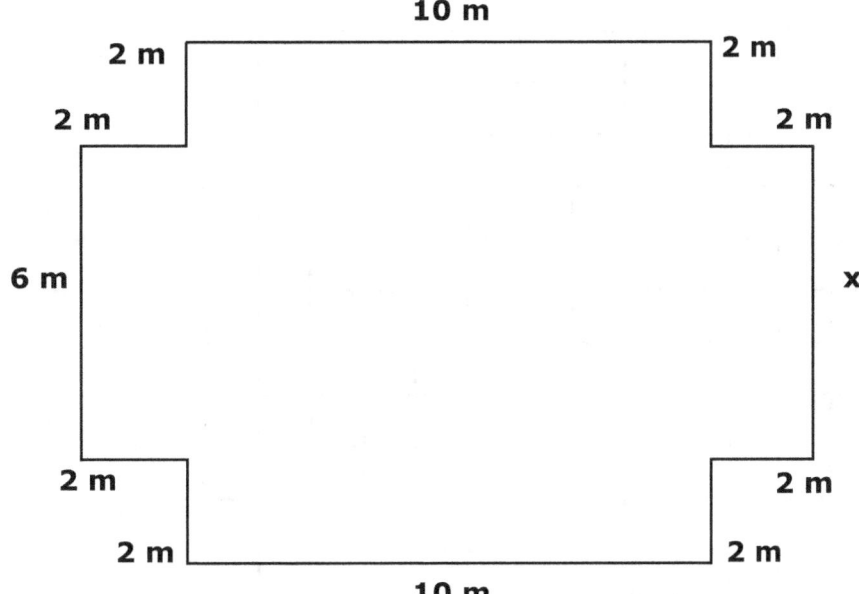

Draw lines to show how the figure could be decomposed to find the total area.

What is the value of X?
- A. 2
- B. 8
- C. 6
- D. 12

MEASUREMENT AND DATA

Explain how you determined the value of X.

_____

_____

What is the total area of the figure?

Answer: _____

12. The school wants to build a garden in the courtyard. Two possible designs for the garden are located on the grid below. Each unit length on the grid equals a length of 1 foot.

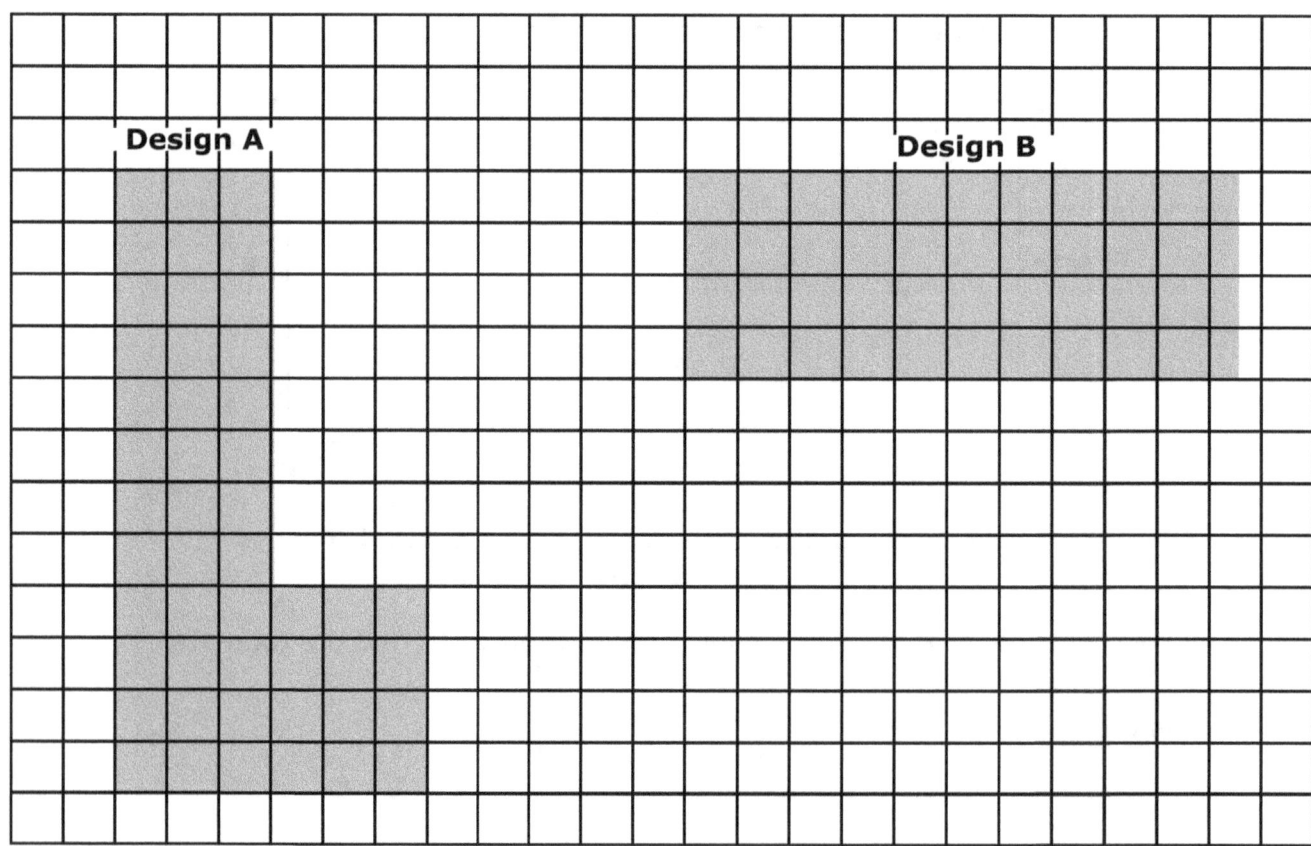

What expression **cannot** be used to find the total area of Design A?

    A. 12 x 4

    B. (12 x 3) + (4 x 3)

    C. (8 x 3) + (6 x 4)

    D. 36 + 12

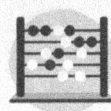

What is the total area of Design A?

Answer: _____

Which design has a greater area? Explain how you know.

_____

_____

_____

_____

MEASUREMENT AND DATA

SOLVE PROBLEMS INVOLVING PERIMETER

3.MD.4.8. Solve real world and mathematical problems involving perimeters of polygons, including finding the perimeter given the side lengths, finding an unknown side length, and exhibiting rectangles with the same perimeter and different areas or with the same area and different perimeters.

1. Find the perimeter of the rectangle below.

   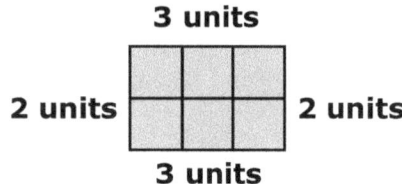

   A. 6 units
   B. 10 units
   C. 5 units
   D. 15 units

2. Find the perimeter of the figure below.

   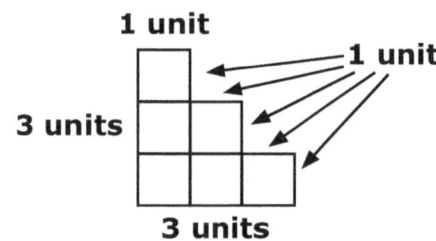

   A. 12 units
   B. 8 units
   C. 6 units
   D. 9 units

3. Find the perimeter of the shaded figure.

   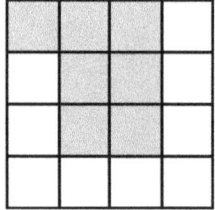

   A. 7 units
   B. 9 units
   C. 12 units
   D. 16 units

4. Find the perimeter of the triangle.

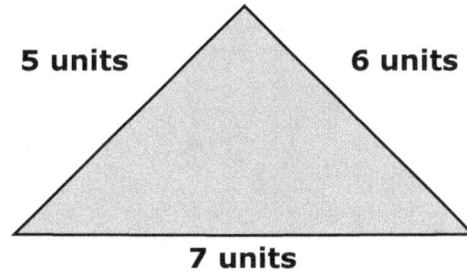

    A. 3 units
    B. 18 units
    C. 16 units
    D. 8 units

5. Which expression could be used to find the perimeter of the shape?

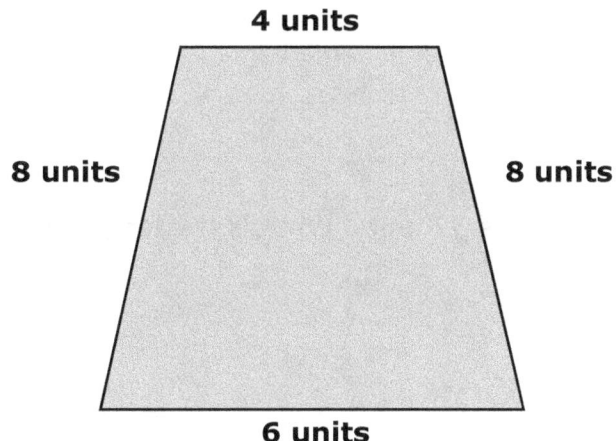

    A. 8 x 4 x 8 x 6
    B. (8 + 4) x (8 + 6)
    C. 8 + 4 + 8 + 6
    D. 16 + 12

What is the perimeter of the trapezoid above?

Answer: _____ units

6. The perimeter of the rectangle is 18 units. What is the length of the missing side?

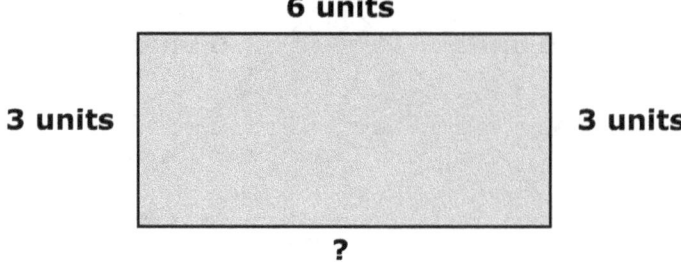

   A. 3 units
   B. 9 units
   C. 6 units
   D. 18 units

7. The computer lab is in the shape of a hexagon. Each side is 30 feet long. What is the perimeter of the computer lab?
   A. 30 feet
   B. 180 feet
   C. 210 feet
   D. 36 feet

8. The perimeter of a rhombus is 32 units. What is the length of each side?
   A. 4 units
   B. 28 units
   C. 32 units
   D. 8 units

9. What is the value of X in the shape below?

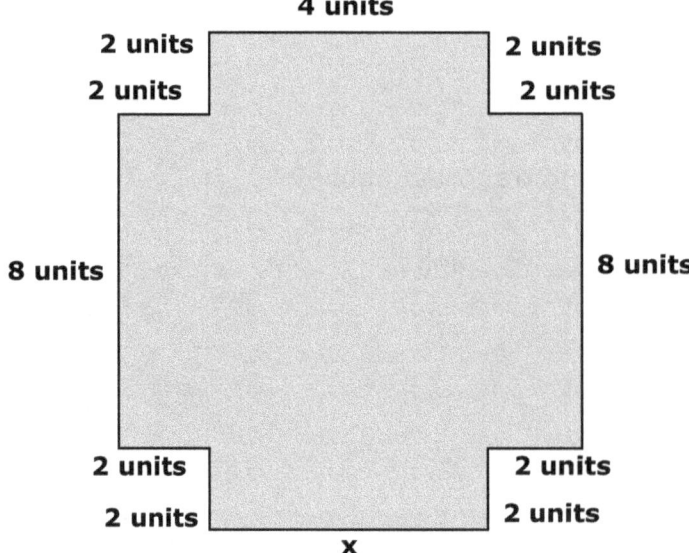

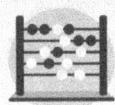

    A. 2
    B. 4
    C. 6
    D. It cannot be determined.

Which expressions can be used to find the total perimeter of the shape above? Choose **ALL** answers that apply.
- [ ] 4 + 2 + 2 + 8 + 2 + 2 + 4 + 2 + 2 + 8 + 2 + 2
- [ ] 4 + 4 + 8 + 4 + 4 + 4 + 8 + 4
- [ ] 6 + 6 + 6 + 6 + 6 + 6
- [ ] 10 + 10 + 6 + 8 + 4 + 2
- [ ] 10 + 10 + 10 + 10
- [ ] 8 + 8 + 4 + 4 + 4 + 6

10. The Third Grade Class is making a large banner for the school's Pep Rally. The banner will be in the shape of a square. They want the perimeter to be between 90 and 100 feet. How many feet across can the banner be? Choose **ALL** answers that apply.
    - [ ] 100 feet
    - [ ] 25 feet
    - [ ] 15 feet
    - [ ] 23 feet
    - [ ] 50 feet
    - [ ] 24 feet

Suppose the class decides to make a smaller square banner. They would like the width to be 15 feet long. What would the perimeter of the banner be now?
    A. 15 feet
    B. 30 feet
    C. 45 feet
    D. 60 feet

What would the area of the banner be if the width was 15 feet long?
    A. 15 feet
    B. 200 feet
    C. 225 feet
    D. 125 feet

MEASUREMENT AND DATA

11. Debbie is baking a cake that needs to have a perimeter of 48 inches. The shape of the cake can be a square, rectangle, or hexagon. What are some of the possible designs she can choose? Choose **ALL** answers that apply.

☐ 20 inches / 4 inches

☐ 17 inches / 7 inches

☐ 8 inches / 6 inches

☐ 8 inches / 8 inches

☐ 12 inches / 12 inches

Debbie decides she would like to make a cake in the shape of a hexagon. How long must each side be to have a total perimeter of 48 inches?

Answer: _____ inches

Explain how you know how long each side must be.

_____

_____

_____

_____

118 MEASUREMENT AND DATA

12. Use the shape below to answer the following questions.

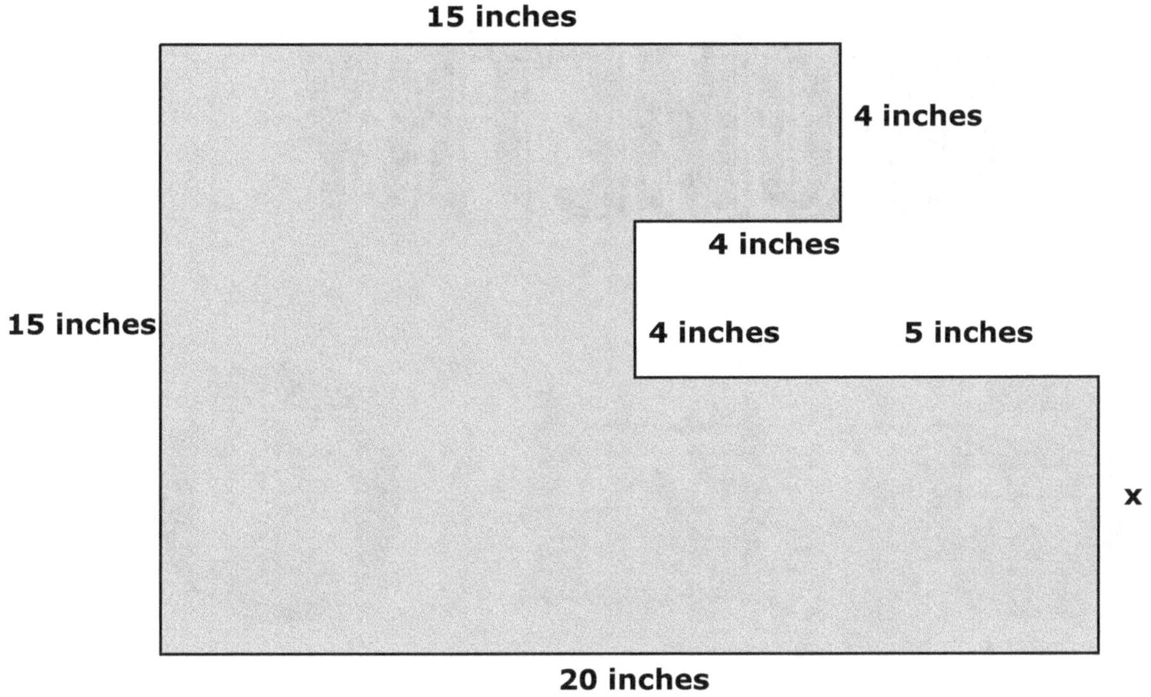

What is the value of X?
 A. 4 units
 B. 6 units
 C. 15 units
 D. 7 units

Draw lines to show how the figure could be decomposed to find the total area.

What is the total area of the figure above?

Answer: _____ square units

What is the total perimeter of the figure above?

Answer: _____ units

How much greater is the area than the perimeter?

Answer: _____ units

GEOMETRY

 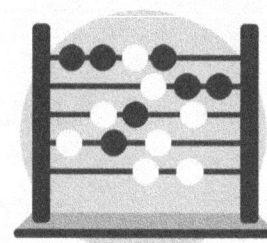 

RECOGNIZE & UNDERSTAND SHAPE CATEGORIES & ATTRIBUTES

3.G.1.1. Understand that shapes in different categories (e.g., rhombuses, rectangles, and others) may share attributes (e.g., having four sides), and that the shared attributes can define a larger category (e.g., quadrilaterals). Recognize rhombuses, rectangles, and squares as examples of quadrilaterals, and draw examples of quadrilaterals that do not belong to any of these subcategories.

1. Which shape below is an example of a quadrilateral?

   A.
   B.

   C.
   D.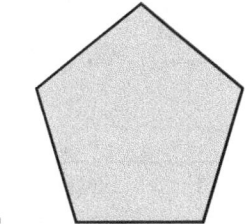

2. Which shape below is NOT an example of a quadrilateral?

   A.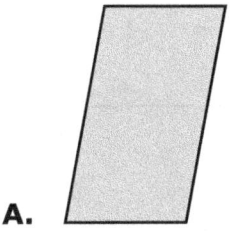
   B.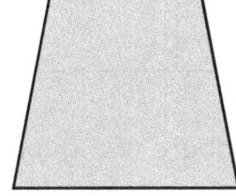

   C.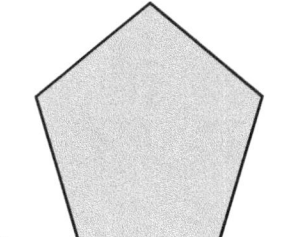
   D.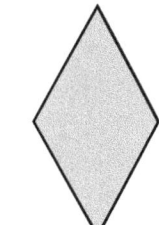

GEOMETRY

3. Sort the shapes below into two categories: quadrilaterals and non-quadrilaterals. Write the letter of each shape into the correct category.

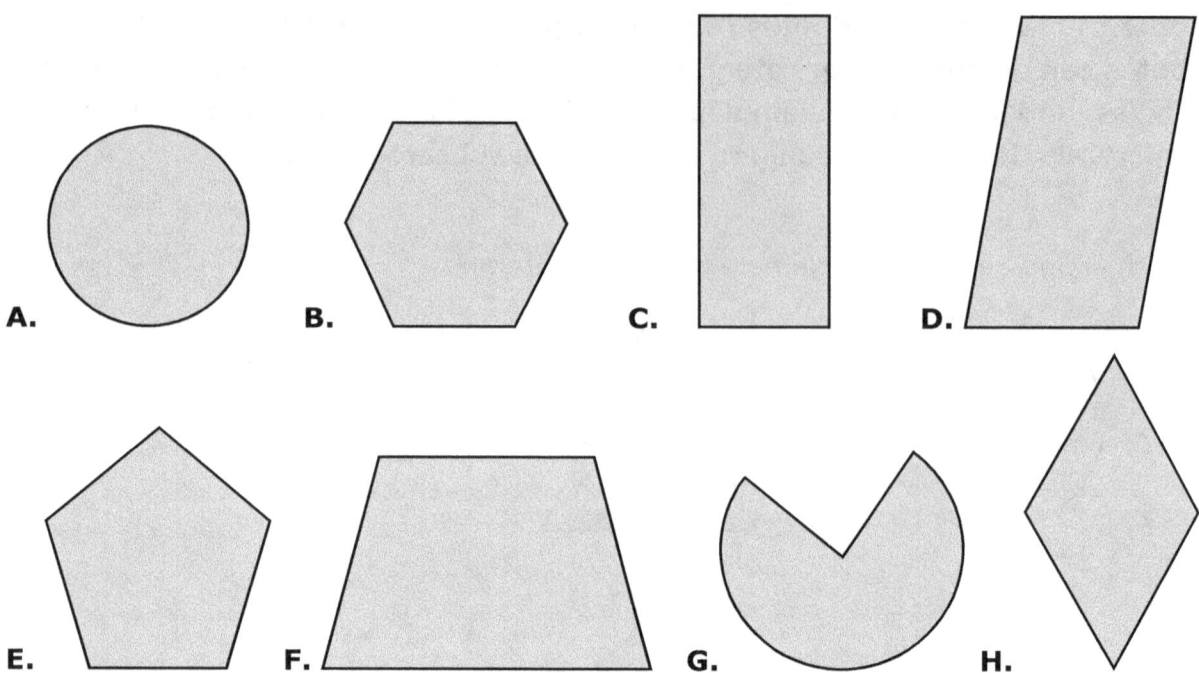

Quadrilaterals	Non-Quadrilaterals

4. Which of the following MUST be an attribute of a quadrilateral? Choose **ALL** that apply.
    - [ ] 4 sides
    - [ ] Curved edges
    - [ ] Closed figure
    - [ ] All sides equal
    - [ ] 4 corners
    - [ ] All square corners

5. Which of the following statements is true?
   A. A triangle has more sides than a quadrilateral.
   B. A rectangle has more sides than a trapezoid.
   C. A parallelogram is not a quadrilateral.
   D. All rhombuses are quadrilaterals.

6. What is the name of the shape below?

   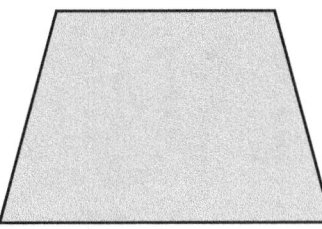

   A. square
   B. rectangle
   C. trapezoid
   D. pentagon

7. What is the name of the shape that has 4 square corners, has 2 lines of symmetry, and has equal opposite sides?
   A. square
   B. rectangle
   C. trapezoid
   D. rhombus

8. What is the name of the shape below?

   A. kite
   B. trapezoid
   C. diamond
   D. parallelogram

   Which of the following are necessary attributes of the shape you selected in the answer above? Choose **ALL** that apply.
   ☐ All sides equal
   ☐ 4 sides
   ☐ Opposite sides equal
   ☐ 4 corners
   ☐ Opposite sides parallel
   ☐ All square corners

GEOMETRY

9. Erin says that all quadrilaterals are squares. Joy says that all squares are quadrilaterals. Who is correct? Explain your answer using pictures and words.

_____

_____

_____

_____

_____

10. Complete the following sentence:

   Rhombuses, squares, and rectangles _____.

   A. all have equal sides.
   B. all have 4 lines of symmetry.
   C. are all parallelograms.
   D. are all congruent.

11. Which of the following statements is true?
   A. All squares are rectangles.
   B. All rectangles are squares.
   C. All rhombuses are squares.
   D. All rhombuses are rectangles.

12. What kind of quadrilateral is shown below? Choose **ALL** answers that apply.

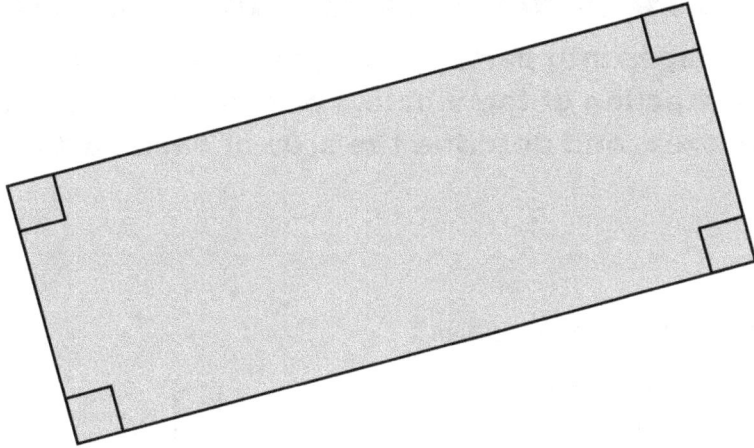

☐ Parallelogram
☐ Square
☐ Rhombus
☐ Trapezoid
☐ Quadrilateral
☐ Rectangle

Draw an example of a quadrilateral that has the same attributes as the shape above.

PARTITION SHAPES & REPRESENT PARTS AS FRACTIONS

3.G.1.2. Partition shapes into parts with equal areas. Express the area of each part as a unit fraction of the whole. For example, partition a shape into 4 parts with equal area, and describe the area of each part as ¼ of the area of the shape.

1. Which figure is divided into equal parts?

   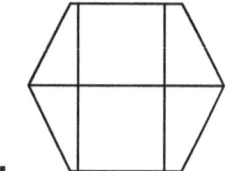
   A.   B.

   C.   D.

2. What fraction of the star is shaded?

   A. $\frac{1}{3}$
   B. $\frac{1}{5}$
   C. $\frac{1}{2}$
   D. 1

3. Which rectangle has $\frac{1}{3}$ of its area shaded?

   A.
   B.
   C.
   D.

GEOMETRY

4. Which shapes show fourths or quarters? Choose **ALL** that apply.

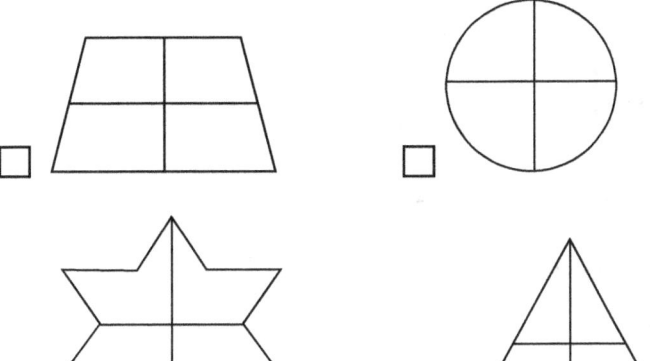

Choose one of the shapes you chose from above and explain how you know it is partitioned into fourths.

_____

_____

_____

_____

5. Partition the shape below to show thirds.

Shade the shape above to show $2/3$.

6. What fraction is each part of the shape below?

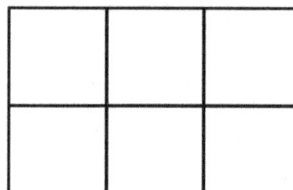

A. 6
B. ¹⁄₆
C. ⁶⁄₆
D. ⁶⁄₁

7. What fraction is each part of the shape below?

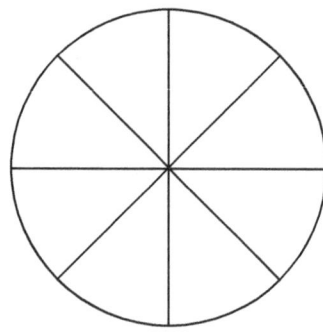

A. ¹⁄₈
B. 1
C. 8
D. ⁸⁄₈

Shade the shape above to show the fraction ³⁄₈.

8. What fraction of the shape below is shaded? Choose **ALL** answers that apply.

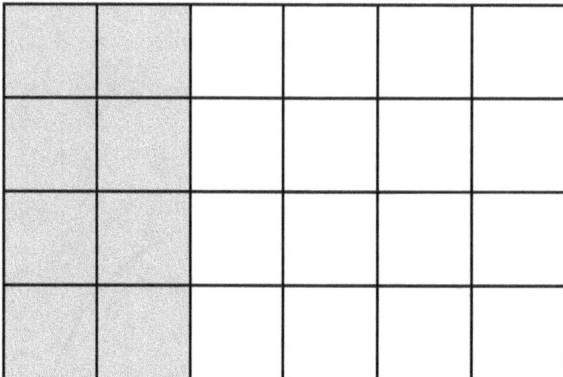

☐ ⁸⁄₂₄
☐ ²⁄₈
☐ ¹⁄₃
☐ ¹⁄₂
☐ ²⁄₆
☐ ⁴⁄₁₂

9. The area of the rectangle is 60 square units. What is the area of one-third of the rectangle?

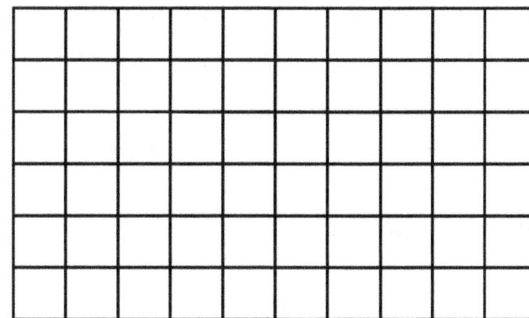

   A. $1/3$
   B. 20 square units
   C. 30 square units
   D. $3/60$

10. The area of the entire rectangle below is 54 square feet. What is the area of the shaded portion?

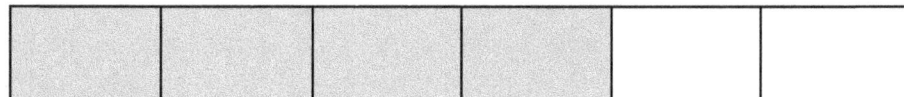

   A. 24 square feet
   B. 4 square feet
   C. 6 square feet
   D. 36 square feet

11. The area of the entire rectangle below is 72 square feet. What is the area of the shaded portion?

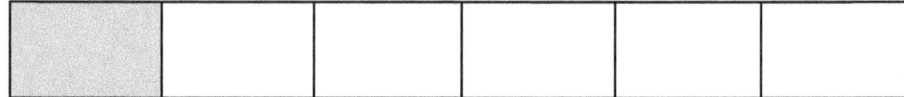

   A. 1 square foot
   B. 12 square feet
   C. 6 square feet
   D. 15 square feet

How many **more** parts of the rectangle above need to be shaded to show an area of 48 square feet?

   A. 1 part
   B. 2 parts
   C. 3 parts
   D. 4 parts

12. The area of the entire rectangle below is 120 square feet.

   Shade the rectangle to show an area of 75 square feet.

   Explain how you know how many parts of the rectangle to shade.

ANSWER KEY

 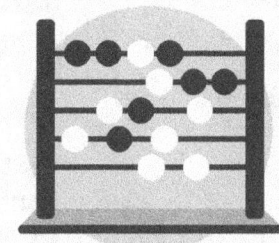 

OPERATIONS & ALGEBRAIC THINKING
3.OA.A.1. Understand Multiplication

1. **C.** The pictorial representation shows an array of 3 rows of stars with 3 stars in each row. To determine the total number of stars altogether, you need to multiply the number of rows of stars and the number of stars in each row: 3 x 3 = N

2. **A, B, D.** The pictorial representation shows an array of 4 rows of desks with 6 desks in each row. To determine the total number of desks altogether, you can use repeated addition or multiplication.

6 + 6 + 6 + 6 or 4 + 4 + 4 + 4 + 4 + 4 can both be used to find the total number of desks.

6 x 4 or 4 x 6 can both be used to find the total number of desks.

3. **A.** 9 x 3 = 27.

Students may mistakenly choose letter B if they divide, letter C if they subtract, or letter D if they add.

4. **Correct array: 35** This question can be worth 2 points: 1 point for a correct array and 1 point for the correct product.

Students can draw an array of objects that contains 5 rows with 7 objects in each row.

For example:

X X X X X X X
X X X X X X X
X X X X X X X
X X X X X X X
X X X X X X X

5 x 7 = 35

5. **D.** 3 bowls of bananas times 6 bananas in each bowl:

3 x 6 = 18 bananas

Students may choose letter A if they incorrectly add, letter B or letter C if they multiply or look too quickly at the question/answers.

6. **B, D. Appropriate explanation.** This question can be worth 2 points: 1 point for the correct answer and 1 point for an appropriate explanation.

6 bookshelves with 7 books on each shelf:

6 x 7 = 42 books

OR 7 + 7 + 7 + 7 + 7 + 7

Students may choose letter A if they add or letter C if they incorrectly multiply or look too quickly at the question/answers.

7. 9, 9, 18

9 x 2 = 18 *or*

2 x 9 = 18

This question can be worth 2 points: 1 point for the correct missing numbers and 1 point for an accurate multiplication sentence.

The repeated addition number sentence that must be used to solve this problem according to the blank squares is 9 + 9 = 18. Students may choose to write this as 9 x 2 or 2 x 9 because of the commutative property. (You can change the order of the factors in a multiplication equation and it will not change the product.)

8. **D.** In order to solve this problem, students must first determine how many miles Danny runs in 1 week. Students must also know that there are 7 days in a week.

3 x 7 = 21

Next, students have to determine how many miles Danny runs in 2 weeks. They can do this by doubling 21 or multiplying it by 2.

21 x 2 = 42

Students may choose answer letter A if they only figure out how many miles Danny runs in one week.

Students may choose answer letter C if they multiply the number of miles Danny runs each day and mutiply by '2' weeks:

3 x 2 = 6

9. **A, C.** Students should use the guess and check strategy to solve this problem by trying each answer choice to see if it works. In order to determine the correct answers, students must multiply the number in the answer choice by 4 (the number of legs on each elephant.) Correct answers will have a product anywhere between 35 and 40.

A. 10 x 4 = 40

B. 8 x 4 = 32

C. 9 x 4 = 36

D. 7 x 4 = 28

10. **A, D, 15 cups.** This question can be worth 3 points: 1 point for the correct number of cups Shane needs to sell in order to earn $5.00, 1 point for the correct number of cups Shane sold over 2 days, and 1 point for the correct number of cups he still needs to sell.

Students should use the guess and check strategy to solve this problem by trying each answer choice to see if it works. In order to determine the correct answer, students must multiply the number in the answer choice by 10 (the cost per cup of lemonade). Correct answers will show a product of 500 ($5.00)

    A. 50 × 10 = 500
    B. 5 × 10 = 50
    C. 10 × 10 = 100
    D. 100 × 10 = 1,000

Shane needs to sell 50 cups in order to make $5.00.

Students can use this same strategy for the 2nd part of the question. In order to determine how many cups of lemonade Shane has sold in 2 days, students must multiply the number in the answer choice by 10 (the cost per cup of lemonade). Correct answers will show a product of 350 ($3.50)

    A. 70 × 10 = 700
    B. 7 × 10 = 70
    C. 5 × 10 = 50
    D. 35 × 10 = 350

Shane sold 35 cups of lemonade which is a total of $3.50.

In order to determine how many more cups of lemonade Shane needs to sell in order to reach his $5.00 goal, students need to subtract the total number of cups from the first two answers: 50 – 35 = 15 cups.

11. **B.** To determine the correct answer, students need to multiply the number of touchdowns each team scored by 7 (the number of points each touchdown is worth.)

    Patriots: 8 touchdowns × 7 = 56
    Giants: 6 touchdowns × 7 = 42

12. **B, D.** To determine how many wheels Richard saw on the cars, you first need to find out how many cars Richard saw altogether: 5 + 5 + 6 + 1 + 1 = 18 cars.

Next, you need to multiply the number of cars, 18, by the number of wheels on each car, 4: 18 × 4 = 72 wheels.

To determine how many wheels Richard saw altogether, including the tractor trailers, you first need to find out how many tractor trailers Richard saw altogether: 2 + 1 + 1 = 4 tractor trailers. Next, you need to multiply the number of tractor trailers, 4, by the number of wheels on each tractor trailer, 18: 4 × 18 = 72 wheels. To find the overall total, you need to add the number of tractor trailer wheels to the number of car wheels: 72 + 72 = 144 wheels altogether.

3.OA.A.2 Understand Division

1. **C.** Letter C is the correct answer because the question is asking to identify how many equal groups there are. This is the only expression that arrives at a solution of 3 equal groups.

2. **A.** Letter A is the correct answer because the question is asking to identify how many hearts are in each group. This is the only expression that arrives at a solution of 6 hearts in each group.

3. **D.** Letter D is the correct answer because 6 ÷ 3 = 2. Students may incorrectly choose letter A if they subtract, or letter C if they add.

4. **Correct model; 4** This question can be worth 2 points: 1 point for drawing a correct model and 1 point for the correct quotient.

Students should draw a model that shows 3 groups of 4 objects for a total of 12 objects altogether.

For example:

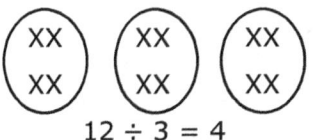

12 ÷ 3 = 4

5. **B.** 40 pizzas divided by 8 slices in each pizza equals 5 pizzas altogether.

    40 ÷ 8 = 5

Students may incorrectly choose letter A if they add or letter D if they subtract.

6. **3rd and 5th choice.** This problem can be solved by using division or addition.

1st choice is an incorrect division statement because it does not correlate with the 16 total tomato plants and the 4 equal rows mentioned in the problem.

3rd and 5th choice are correct because both have a solution of 4 tomato plants in each row.

7. **1st and 2nd choice; 7 days** This problem can be solved by using division or repeated subtraction.

3rd Choice is an incorrect division statement because it does not correlate with the 63 total pages and 9 pages read each day as mentioned in the problem.

1st and 2nd Choice are correct because both have a solution of 7 days.

8. **A.** In order to determine the correct answer, you need to divide the total number of dollars Katie earned by the number of dollars she earns each day:

    30 ÷ 5 = 6

Students may incorrectly choose letter C if they subtract or letter D if they add.

Letter B is an incorrect division statement because

it does not correlate with the 30 total dollars Katie earned and the number of dollars she earns each day (5).

9. **D; Appropriate explanation.** This question can be worth 2 points: 1 point for the correct total number of pieces of candy per friend and 1 point for an appropriate explanation.

First, students need to determine how many pieces of candy Jack has to share after keeping 22 pieces for himself: 132 − 22 = 110.

Next, students need to divide the total number of pieces of candy left by the 10 friends he is going to share with:

110 ÷ 10 = 11 pieces of candy per friend;

No, Jack will not have any pieces of candy leftover. This is because 110 ÷ 10 = 11. This means that each friend gets 11 pieces of candy and there will not be any pieces of candy leftover.

10. **B; 4; A.** In order to determine how many cartons of eggs Auntie Ava will need, students need to divide the total number of eggs she needs, 32, by the total number of eggs in each carton, 12.

32 ÷ 12 = 2 with 8 leftover

Auntie Ava will need 3 cartons because there will not be enough eggs in only 2 cartons (24).

There are 36 eggs in 3 cartons. Auntie Ava only needs 32. Therefore, there will be 4 eggs leftover.

36 − 32 = 4

If Auntie Ava doubles the recipe, she will now need 64 eggs. In order to determine how many cartons of eggs she will need now, students need to divide 64 by the total number of eggs in each carton, 12.

64 ÷ 12 = 5 with 4 leftover

Auntie Ava will need 6 cartons because there will not be enough eggs in only 5 cartons (60).

11. **19; $190; 2.** First, students will need to determine how many people are going on the field trip altogether: 86 + 7 = 93.

Next, students need to divide how many people are going on the trip altogether, 93, by how many people can fit in each van, 5.

93 ÷ 5 = 18 with 3 remaining

They will need 19 vans because there will not be enough room in only 18 vans (90).

To determine the total cost of the vans, students need to multiply the total number of vans, 19, by the cost of each van, $10.

19 × 10 = $190

To determine how much each student ticket costs, students first need to determine how much money was spent on the adult tickets.

If 7 adults went on the trip and each adult ticket costs $4, then students need to multiply:

7 × 4 = $28.

Next, students need to determine how much money was left after purchasing the adult tickets:

200 − 28 = $172.

Last, students need to divide the amount of money left, $172 by the number of students, 86:

172 ÷ 86 = 2

12. **$15; $35; Yes**. In order to determine how much each pizza costs, students first need to determine how much money was spent on pizza altogether. This can be figured out by subtracting how much money Mr. Clark started with and how much money he was left with: 100 − 55 = 45.

Next, students need to divide how much money Mr. Clark spent on pizza by how many pizzas he bought: 45 ÷ 3 = 15.

To determine how much money Mr. Clark has left after buying ice cream cones, students need to first determine how much money Mr. Clark spent on ice cream: 5 cones times $4 per cone = $20.00

Next, students need to subtract how much money Mr. Clark spent on ice cream by how much money he had left over from the pizza: $55 - $20 = $35

To determine if Mr. Clark has enough money to buy $25.00 of gas, students need to look at how much money he had left after purchasing ice cream and pizza: $35. Therefore, Mr. Clark does have enough money left over to buy $25 of gas.

Students must appropriately explain how they know Mr. Clark has enough money to buy gas. For example:

Yes, Mr. Clark has enough money to buy gas. I know this because he had $35 leftover after buying pizza and ice cream. Therefore, he has enough money to buy $25 of gas.

OA.A.3. Use Multiplication & Division to Solve Word Problems

1. **C.** The clue words *each* and *altogether* indicate that repeated addition/multiplication is required to answer the question. 3 × 12 = 36 cookies

3 + 3 + 3 + 3 + 3 + 3 + 3 + 3 + 3 + 3 + 3 + 3 = 36 cookies

2. **B.** The clue words each and total cost indicate that repeated addition/multiplication is required to answer the question.

$$10 \times 5 = c$$

3. $72 \div 9 = r$

r = 8.

Colin has 72 seeds to plant altogether. If he wants to place 9 seeds in each row, you must divide to determine how many rows Colin will need to plant. 72 seeds divided into rows of 9 seeds each means that Colin will need to plant 8 rows altogether.

4. **A.** Lila needs $48. If she earns $6 per week, she will need to do chores for 8 weeks before she can buy the video game. This problem can be solved in a variety of ways. The most efficient way to solve the problem is through a division equation: $48 \div 6 = 8$

Students can also create a chart using a skip counting pattern:

WEEK #	1	2	3	4	5	6	7	8
$ EARNED	6	6	6	6	6	6	6	6

5. **D.** The clue words each and total number indicate that repeated addition/multiplication is required to answer the question.

$$11 \times 4 = p$$

6. **B.** Letter B is the only possible answer choice because $12 \times 5 = 60$ and Lila has 60 apple chunks altogether.

Letter A is not correct because $3 \times 15 = 45$
Letter C is not correct because $2 \times 15 = 30$
Letter D is not correct because $10 \times 5 = 50$

7. **B.** First, you need to determine how many people are going to the zoo altogether:

2 adults + 3 children = 5 people altogether.

Next, you need to multiply the number of people going to the zoo times the cost of each ticket:

5 people x $7 per ticket = $35

8. **Yes, Emmi is correct.** This question can be worth 2 points: 1 point for having the correct answer, Emmi is correct, and 1 point for having a specific explanation. An appropriate explanation should include a connection to division. For example, I know Emmi is correct because there are 21 students altogether. If each pizza has 9 slices and each student is only having 1 slice, I can divide 21 by 9 to determine how many pizzas the class will need.

$21 \div 9 = 2$ pizzas with remainder of 3.

Therefore 2 pizzas are not enough and the class will need 3 pizzas.

9. **1st and 5th Choice.** First, you need to determine how many pieces of chocolate Omar starts with: 4 boxes of chocolate times 9 pieces of chocolate in each box equals 36 pieces of chocolate altogether.

Next, you need to subtract the number of pieces of chocolate that Omar shared with his friends.

$$36 - 12 = 24 \text{ pieces of chocolate}$$

The equations in both the *1st choice* and *5th choice* can be used to solve this problem correctly.

10. **8 vans.** Students can solve this problem in a variety of ways. They can draw a picture, create a chart, or write an equation.

The equations used to solve this problem correctly are:

26 girls + 22 boys = 48 students altogether

48 students are then divided into groups of 6.

48 students divided into groups of 6 students per van = 8 vans altogether

A chart can also be used to solve this problem after students have added 26 girls + 22 boys = 48 students altogether.

# OF VANS	1	2	3	4	5	6	7	8
# OF STUDENTS PER VAN	6	6	6	6	6	6	6	6
TOTAL # OF STUDENTS	6	12	18	24	30	36	42	48

11. **D.** Choice D is the correct answer because 3 tables of 4 can fit 12 people, and 7 tables of 6 can fit 42 people. When the totals are added together, $12 + 42 = 54$ people altogether. This is correct because this seating arrangement can fit 54 people, which is the total number of people attending the party.

Choice A is not correct because:
$4 \times 4 = 16$ and $8 \times 6 = 48$, so $16 + 48 = 64$

Choice B is not correct because:
$6 \times 4 = 24$ and $4 \times 6 = 24$, so $24 + 24 = 48$

Choice C is not correct because:
$5 \times 4 = 20$ and $5 \times 6 = 30$, so $20 + 30 = 50$

12. **B.** First, you need to determine how many pieces of construction paper were ordered per grade level.

Grade 3: 3 packs of 24 sheets: $3 \times 24 = 72$ sheets
Grade 4: 2 packs of 12 sheets: $2 \times 12 = 24$ sheets
Grade 5: 2 packs of 28 sheets: $2 \times 18 = 36$ sheets

Second, you need to determine how many sheets were ordered altogether by adding the total number of sheets ordered for each grade level:

$$72 + 24 + 36 = 132 \text{ sheets.}$$

3.OA.A.4. Find Unknown Values in Multiplication/Division Equations

1. **A.** The illustration shows 2 rows of smiley faces and 4 smiley faces in each row. Therefore, 2 x 4 = 8.

2. **C.** The illustration shows 3 rows of stars and 5 stars in each row. Therefore, 3 x 5 = 15.

3. **D.** The illustration shows 5 rows of triangles and 4 triangles in each row. Therefore, 20 ÷ 5 = 4

4. **Correct array: 6.** This question can be worth 2 points: 1 point for drawing a correct array and 1 point for completing the number sentence correctly.

The array should show 5 rows of objects with 6 objects in each row for a total of 30 objects. For example:

$$X\ X\ X\ X\ X\ X$$
$$X\ X\ X\ X\ X\ X$$
$$X\ X\ X\ X\ X\ X$$
$$X\ X\ X\ X\ X\ X$$
$$X\ X\ X\ X\ X\ X$$
$$30 ÷ 5 = N$$
$$N = 6$$

5. **C.** The only number that can correctly complete each number sentence is 3.

$$21 ÷ N = 7$$
$$21 ÷ 3 = 7$$
$$N \times 4 = 12$$
$$3 \times 4 = 12$$
$$N ÷ 1 = 3$$
$$3 ÷ 1 = 3$$

6. **8.**

$$9 \times N = 72$$
$$N = 8$$

7. **Input: 6, Output: 10, Rule: multiplying by 2.**

This question can be worth 3 points: 1 point for the correct Input number, 1 point for the correct Output number, and 1 point for identifying the correct rule.

The rule in this table is multiplying by 2: take the number that you are inputting and multiply it by 2. Or, in the reverse, take the number you are outputting and divide it by 2. Therefore, the missing Input number is 6 because 12 ÷ 2 = 6. The missing Output number is 10 because 5 x 2 = 10.

Depending on how students see the table, they may explain the rule is multiplying by 2, dividing by 2, or both. All should be considered correct.

8. **2nd and 3rd Choices.** The key words *in each pie* tell us to divide the total number of apples by the total number of pies: 18 ÷ 3.

This can also be solved by using multiplication: 3 x what number = 18?

The 1st choice is an incorrect division statement because it does not correlate with the total 18 apples and the 3 pies mentioned in the problem.

9. **48; Appropriate explanation.** This question can be worth 2 points: 1 point for the correct answer and 1 point for an appropriate explanation.

$$N ÷ 8 = 6$$
$$48 ÷ 8 = 6$$

An example of an appropriate student explanation is:

Multiplication can help me solve this problem because I know that multiplication and division are opposites. I know that multiplication and division make a fact family. I know that 6 x 8 = 48. Therefore, I know 48 ÷ 8 = 6.

10. **B.** This question is asking students to determine what numbers can be multiplied by 6 to have a product less than 30. This requires students to carefully look at each answer choice.

Letter B is correct because: 2 x 6 = 12, 3 x 6 = 18, and 4 x 6 = 24.
Letter C is incorrect because 6 x 6 = 36.
Letter D is incorrect because 6 x 6 = 36 and 6 x 7 = 42.

11. **3rd & 4th choices; 1st & 2nd Choices.** Gabe has 90 baseball cards. Each page in the album can hold 5 or 6 cards. This means you need to divide 90 by 5 and by 6 to determine the possible number of pages he will need.

$$90 ÷ 5 = 18$$
$$90 ÷ 6 = 15$$

Next, Gabe gets 30 baseball cards for his birthday and wants to put them in the same album. This means you need to divide 30 by 5 and 6 to determine how many MORE pages he will need.

$$30 ÷ 5 = 6$$
$$30 ÷ 6 = 5$$

12. **$23, 8 cookies, 6 cookies; Appropriate explanation.** This question can be worth 4 points: 1 point for each correct answer and 1 point for an appropriate explanation.

To determine how much money Max raised, you need to first multiply the number Oatmeal Raisin Cookies he sold by the cost of each cookie: 2 x 4 = 8. Next you need to multiply the number of Peanut Butter Cookies he sold by the cost of each cookie: 3 x 5 = 15. Last, you need to add these two costs together: 15 + 8 = $23.00

In order to determine how many cookies Wendy sold, you need to divide the amount of money she made by the cost of each cookie: 32 ÷ 4 = 8 cookies.

In order to determine the greatest number of cookies Mrs. Miller could have bought, you need to divide the amount of money she has by the cost of each cookie: 20 ÷ 3 = 6 cookies with 2 dollars leftover.

An appropriate explanation should refer to the student's thought process and the math that they used to solve the problem. For example:

The greatest number of Peanut Butter Cookies that Mrs. Miller can buy is 6. I know this because each Peanut Butter Cookie costs $3 and 3 x 6 = 18. Mrs. Miller cannot buy 7 Peanut Butter Cookies because that would cost $21. So, Mrs. Miller will have 2 dollars left over.

3.OA.B.5. Know and Use Properties of Multiplication & Division

1. **C.** These models are examples of the Commutative Property. The Commutative Property states that you can switch the order of the factors you are multiplying, but your product will remain the same. Both models of a product of 20. The first model shows 5 x 4 and the second model shows 4 x 5.

2. **A.** This number sentence is an example of the Associative Property. The Associative Property states that you can group the factors you are multiplying in different ways, but your product will remain the same. This model shows 3 arrays and each array is 2 rows of 2. Therefore, the product is 12.

3. **D; See detailed explanation for model.**

This number sentence is an example of the Distributive Property. The Distributive Property states that you can multiply each addend separately and then add the products together to get a total sum. The model shows 3 x 8, but students are asked to draw a line that represents the Distributive Property using the equation: (3 x 2) + (3 x 6); Therefore, students must draw a line to create a 3 x 2 array and a 3 x 6 array. Altogether, the answer is 24.

4. **8, 40, 20, 40.** This examples represent the Associative Property.

2 x 4 x 5 = (2 x 4) x 5   2 x 4 x 5 = 2 x (4 x 5)
         = **8** x 5   = 2 x **20**
         = **40**   = **40**

When factors appear in parenthesis, they must be multiplied before anything else. In the first example, students need to multiply the 2 and the 4, which then transforms the equation into 8 x 5, which has a product of 40. In the second example, students need to multiply 4 x 5, which then transforms the equation into 2 x 20, which also has a product of 40. Therefore, it doesn't matter how you group the factors, the product will remain the same.

5. **No; Appropriate explanation.** This question can be worth 2 points: 1 point for the correct answer and 1 point for an appropriate explanation. This question measures student understanding of the Zero Property. The Zero Property states that any factor times zero always equals zero. Therefore, Karen is incorrect. An appropriate explanation should yield to the Zero Property. For example:

Karen is incorrect. I know this because the Zero Property says that any number times zero is zero. Therefore, 5 x 0 is 0.

6. **2nd and 3rd Choices.** This question can be worth 2 points: 1 point for each correct answer.

This question is used to measure student understanding of the Associative Property. The 2nd choice and 3rd choice are the correct answers because they group the factors in different ways, but the product remains the same.

4 x 3 x 2 =
(3 x 2) x 4: multiply the factors in parenthesis first, 3 x 2 = 6 and 6 x 4 = 24

(4 x 3) x 2: multiply the factors in parenthesis first, 4 x 3 = 12 and 12 x 2 = 24

7. **D.** This question is used to measure student understanding of the Distributive Property. The line divides the larger array of 3 x 11 into 2 smaller arrays. The array on the left side of the line shows 3 x 3, and the array on the right side of the line shows 3 x 8.

8. **No; Appropriate explanation.** This question can be worth 2 points: 1 point for the correct answer and 1 point for an appropriate explanation.

This question asks students to apply their understanding of the Commutative Property. The Commutative Property only applies to Addition and Mulitplication. Therefore, the equations **27 ÷ 3 = 9** and **9 ÷ 3 = 27** do not mean the same thing. An appropriate explanation should yield student understanding of the Commutative Property. For example:

No, I do not agree with Alex. I do not agree with Alex because the Commutative Property only works for Addition and Multiplication. Also, I know that 9 divided by 3 is 3, not 27.

9. **1st, 3rd and 4th Choices;** 36 cookies. This question can be worth 4 points: 1 point for each correct answer.

This question asks students to apply the Associative Property into a word problem. To determine the total number of cookies, you need to multiply 2, 3, and 6. 1st, 3rd and 4th Choice use the Associative Property in different ways, but still have the same product.

1st Choice: (2 x 3) x 6. Multiply factors in parenethsis first, so 2 x 3 equals 6, and 6 x 6 = 36.

3rd Choice: 6 x 6. This equation works because after you multiply the 2 and 3 in parenthesis, the equation you are left with is 6 x 6 = 36.

4th Choice: 18 x 2. This question works because the Associative Property means that you can also group the factors as (6 x 3) x 2, and in doing so, you would be left with 18 x 2 = 36.

10. **See detailed explanation.** This question can be worth 3 points: 1 point for each correct match.

Students should draw a line that matches 9 x 7 and (7 x 3) + (7 x 6). This works because if you multiply the numbers in parenthesis first, you get 21 + 42 = 63 and 9 x 7 = 63.

Students should draw a line that matches 6 x 8 and (8 x 4) + (8 x 2). This works because if you multiply the numbers in parethesis first, you get 32 + 16 = 48 and 6 x 8 = 48.

Students should draw a line that matches 4 x 12 and (4 x 5) + (4 x 7). This works because if you multiply the numbers in parenthesis first, you get 20 + 28 = 48 and 4 x 12 = 48.

11. **1st, 2nd and 3rd Choices; Appropriate explanation.** This question can be worth 4 points: 1 point for each correct answer and 1 point for an appropriate explanation.

This question measures student understanding of applying the Commutative, Associative, and Distributive Properties.

The 1st Choice is correct because it demonstrates correct use of the Commutative Property.

The 2nd Choice is correct because it demonstrates correct use of the Associative Property.

The Third Choice is correct because it demonstrates correct use of the Distributive Property.

An appropriate explanation should yield to student understanding of the property of the letter they have chosen to explain.

For example: I know that the 2nd Choice is correct because it shows how the Associative Property can be used to solve 6 x 7. I know that 6 x 7 = 42. In the equation (2 x 3) x 7, you have to multiply the factors in the parenthesis first: 2 x 3 = 6 and 6 x 7 = 42. The answers are the same.

12. **Appropriate line; C; 50 ft.; Appropriate equation; 126 sq. feet.** This question can be worth 5 points: 1 point for each correct answer.

Before students can determine where to draw the line to divide Mr. Jay's garden, they have to determine which side of the garden should be bigger. Mr. Jay has 6 packages of flower seeds and each package holds between 15 – 20 seeds. Therefore, Mr. Jay has between 90 and 120 flower seeds. He has a box of vegetable plants arranged in 5 rows with 4 plants in each row, so he has 20 plants. Therefore, students need to draw a line demonstrating that one section of the garden is much larger than the other. For example:

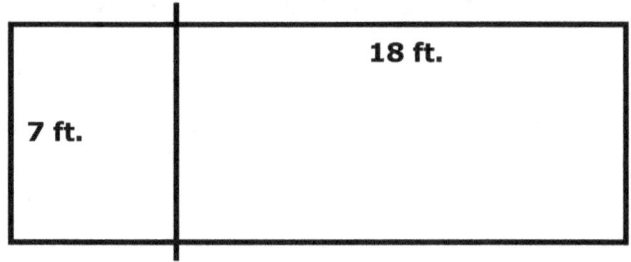

Students should show that one section of the garden is greater than ½ and the other section is smaller than ½.

Next, students need to determine how much total fencing Mr. Jay will need. This asks students to determine the perimeter of the shape. To find the perimeter, students need to add the measurements of each side together: 18 + 18 + 7 + 7 = N. Letter C is correct because it shows that 18 + 18 have been added to equal 36 and 7 + 7 have been added to equal 14. Mr. Jay will need 50 ft. of fencing.

For the last question, students are to demonstrate an understanding of the properties of multiplication. Therefore, they should not be using the equation 18 x 7 to find the total area of the shape. Students should refer to where they drew the line in step 1, to determine the measurements of each smaller rectangle. For example:

This illustration shows how the length of the shape was divided into 6 + 12. The width of the shape remains the same. To find the total area of the shape, students must find the area of each smaller rectangle first and then add them together.

$$6 \times 7 = 42$$
$$12 \times 7 = 84$$
$$84 + 42 = 126 \text{ square ft.}$$

In doing so, students are demonstrating an understanding of the Distributive Property.

If students choose to use the Associative Property, they may break down the length of 18 feet into something smaller such as: 6 x 3. To find the total area then, students would solve (6 x 3) x 7 = 126 square ft.

3.OA.B.6. Find Unknown Factors: Division

1. **C.** This illustration shows 2 groups of 5 circles in each group for a total of 10 stars altogether. Therefore, 10 ÷ 2 = 5 and 5 x 2 = 10.

2. **B.** This question measures the student's ability to identify inverse operations. 21 ÷ 3 = N and 3 x N = 21 mean the same thing.

3. **A.** This model shows 6 rectangles with 4 circles in each rectangle for a total of 24 circles. Therefore, 6 x 4 = 24 and 24 ÷ 6 = 4

4. **D.**   35 ÷ N = 7 and 7 x N = 35
         7 x 5 = 35 and 35 ÷ 5 = 7

5. **A.** The clue words *each student* and *altogether* indicate that you need to multiply. To determine the total number of cookies, you need to multiply the number of students, 5, by how many cookies each student bakes, 12.

   5 x 12 = 60 cookies altogether

6. **C.** This question measures a student's ability to recognize inverse operations.

   4 x N = 36 means the same thing as 36 ÷ 4 = N.

7. **Appropriate explanation; 7.** This question can be worth 2 points: 1 point for an appropriate explanation and 1 point for the correct answer.

An appropriate student explanation should demonstrate an understanding of the relationship between multiplication and division. For example:

Abby could use multiplication to help her solve division because they are opposites. For Abby to solve 42 ÷ 6, she just has to think about 6 times what number equals 42.

6 x N = 42. If Abby knows that 6 x 7 = 42, then she can solve 42 ÷ 6 = 7. N = 7.

8. **See detailed explanation.** This question can be worth 5 points: 1 point for each correct match.

Students should draw a line connecting:

$$24 \div 3 = 8 \text{ and } 8 \times 3 = 24.$$
$$24 \div 6 = 4 \text{ and } 4 \times 6 = 24$$
$$20 \div 5 = 4 \text{ and } 4 \times 5 = 20$$
$$36 \div 3 = 12 \text{ and } 12 \times 3 = 36$$
$$24 \div 2 = 12 \text{ and } 12 \times 2 = 24$$

9. **D; Appropriate explanation.** This question measures a student understanding of fact families as well as inverse operations. Letters A, B, and C are all part of the same fact family, so they can each help solve for 28 ÷ 4.

An appropriate student explanation should demonstrate some understanding of the fact family relationship. For example, I know that 4 ÷ N = 28 cannot be used to help solve 28 ÷ 4 = N. I know this because the number 4 cannot be divided by another number and equal 28. I also know that the 4 equations in this fact family are: 4 x 7 = 28, 7 x 4 = 28, 28 ÷ 7 = 4 and 28 ÷ 4 – 7. Therefore, 4 ÷ N = 28 cannot be used to help solve for 28 ÷ 4.

10. **A, 81 paper plates, NO; Appropriate division sentence; Appropriate multiplication sentence.** This question can be worth 6 points: 1 point for each correct answer, 1 point for an appropriate division sentence, 1 point for an appropriate multiplication sentence, and 1 point for an appropriate explanation.

To determine the total number of paper plates the students will need, you need to multiply the number of students by how many paper plates each student will need: 9 x 9 = 81.

To determine if there are enough straws for the students, you have to first figure out how many straws the students will need altogether. You will need to multiply the number of students 9, by the number of straws each student needs, 4. 9 x 4 = 36.

Students can use either 36 ÷ 9 = 4 or 36 ÷ 4 = 9 as a division number sentence.

Students can use either 4 x 9 = 36 or 9 x 4 = 36 as a multiplication number sentence.

An appropriate student explanation should use at least one of these number sentences to explain their thinking. For example:

I know that the students do not have enough straws. I know this because there are 9 students and each student needs 4 straws. This means they need 36 straws altogether. If they only have 34 straws, they are 2 straws short.

11. Appropriate explanation to support answer, example of multiplication sentence, example of division sentence. This question can be worth 4 points: 1 point for an answer, 1 point for an appropriate explanation to that answer, 1 point for an example of a multiplication sentence, and 1 point for an example of a division sentence.

To demonstrate an understanding of the connection between multiplication and division, it is likely that students will agree with Drew. However, it can be acceptable for students to disagree with Drew, as long as they are able to support their thinking with appropriate evidence. An appropriate student explanation is as follows:

I agree with Drew because multiplication and division are opposites. For example, if I know that 4 x 3 = 12. I can solve the division fact for 12 ÷ 3. I just have to think in my head 3 times what number equals 12.

12. Answers will vary; D; 104 desserts. Student answers for the first part of this question will vary. Any answer is acceptable as long as the seating is used correctly (4 per square, 6 per rectangle, and 10 per circle).

Some possible answers are:

1 squares: (1 x 4 = 4)
3 rectangles: (6 x 3 = 18)
3 circles (10 x 3 = 30)
4 + 18 + 30 = 52

2 squares: (2 x 4 = 8)
4 rectangles: (6 x 4 = 24)
2 circles (10 x 2 = 20)
8 + 24 + 20 = 52

To determine how many desserts the Shu Family will need so that each guest can have 2 desserts, you need to multiply 52 x 2 or add 52 + 52.

52 x 2 = 104. They will need 104 desserts.

3.OA.C.7. Know Relationship between Multiplication & Division

1. **D.** This questions measures student understanding that multiplying any factor times zero equals zero.

2. **A.** Letter A is correct because 25 ÷ 5 = 5.

3. **C.** Letter C is correct because 3 x 7 = 21.

4. **D.** Letter D is correct because 20 ÷ 2 = 10.

5. **See detailed explanation.** This question can be worth 5 points: 1 point for each correct match.

Students should draw a line that matches:

3 x 9 = 27 and 27 ÷ 3 = 9
4 x 3 = 12 and 12 ÷ 4 = 3
5 x 6 = 30 and 30 ÷ 5 = 6
2 x 6 = 12 and 12 ÷ 2 = 6
10 x 3 = 30 and 30 ÷ 10 = 3

6. **A.** A complete fact family includes 2 multiplication number sentences and 2 division number sentences. This fact family is missing a division number sentence. Letter B and Letter C are incorrect because they have the quotient, dividend, and divisor in the wrong location of the number sentence.

7. **A.** This question measures student understanding about dividing by zero. Any number divided by zero equals zero.

8. **4 x 8 = 32**

 8 x 4 = 32

 32 ÷ 4 = 8

 32 ÷ 8 = 4.

This question can be worth 4 points: 1 point for each correct number sentence. A complete fact family has 4 number sentences: 2 multiplication number sentences and 2 division number sentences.

9. **1st, 2nd & 3rd choices.** The 4th Choice is incorrect because any number times zero equals zero.

10. **Correctly filled in chart; 2 patterns explained.** This question can be worth 10 points: 1 point for each correct answer in the table and 1 point for each pattern explained.

÷9	9	18	27	36	45	54
9	**1**	**2**	**3**	**4**	**5**	**6**

Numbers in bold are the correct answers.

Acceptable student responses should clearly explain 2 different patterns. For example:

1 pattern I noticed is that the division table also shows multiplication facts. For example, 18 ÷ 2 = 9 is the same thing as 9 x 2 = 18. Another pattern I noticed is that when you add the digits of each quotient, you get a sum of 9. For example, 18: 1 + 8 = 9 and 27: 2 + 7 = 9.

Students may also say that they notice the pattern is counting up by nines or that the quotients are in a pattern of odd, even, odd, even.

11. **D, A, D.** This question can be worth 3 points: 1 point for each correct answer. To determine how many baskets Kara used, you need to divide the total number of apples she picked, 28, by the total number of apples in each basket, 7. 28 ÷ 7 = 4 baskets.

To determine how many apples Kara's brother picked, you need to multiply the number of baskets, 5, by the number of apples in each basket, 8. 5 x 8 = 40 apples.

To determine how many apples Kara and her brother picked altogether, you need to add the number of apples Kara picked and the number of apples her brother picked: 40 + 28 = 68 apples.

12. **B; yes, $3; Appropriate explanation.** This question can be worth 4 points: 1 point for each correct answer and 1 point for an appropriate explanation.

First, you need to subtract the amount of money James already has and the amount of money he needs to save up to: $62 – $12 = $50.

Next, you need to determine how much money James can earn if he rakes the maximum number of yards on the first day. If he can rake 5 yards and makes $5 for each yard: 5 x 5 = $25.

Next, you have to subtract the amount of money James earns for raking leaves and the amount of money he needs to save up to: $50 - $25 = $25.

James earns $4 a day for doing chores. To determine how many days he will have to do chores, you need to divide: 25 ÷ 4 = 6 remainder 1

This means that James will have to do chores for 7 days. If he only does chores for 6 days, he won't have enough money.

James will have to do chores for 7 days and he will have $3 leftover. An example of an appropriate explanation is as follows:

James will have $1.00 left. I know this because he needs to do his chores until he makes $25.00. If he makes $4.00 a day, he will need to do chores for 7 days. If he only does chores for 6 days, he will only make $24. If James does chores for 7 days, he will earn $28 because 4 x 7 = 28. Therefore, James will have $3 left over because $28 - $25 = $3.

3.OA.D.8. Solve Two-Step Word Problems

1. **C.** To solve this problem, you need to first find out how many strawberries are left after Lila eats 2: 12 – 2 = 10.

Next, you need to find out how many strawberries Lila has left after she shares with her baby sister: 10 – 3 = 7. There are 7 strawberries left.

2. **D.** To solve this problem, you need to first find out how many blueberries Brady has left after he eats 6 of them. 36 – 6 = 30. Next, you need to divide the total number of blueberries he has left, 30, by how many people he is splitting them with, 3, including himself; 30 ÷ 3 = 10.

They will each get 10 blueberries.

3. **A.** Before you can figure out how many tissues were used each day, you need to subtract the total number of tissues that were in the box to start, 50, and the number of tissues that were left at the end of the week, 25. 50 – 25 = t.

4. **B.** First, you need to determine how many cucumbers, 10, and peppers, 6, that Mr. Watters picked. 10 + 6 = 16.

Next, you need to subtract the total number of vegetables Mr. Watters picked, 28, by the number of total cucumbers and peppers, 16.

28 – 16 = 12. This means that Mr. Watters picked 12 tomatoes.

5. **A, $28.** This question can be worth 2 points: 1 point for each correct answer.

To determine how much money Joe has left after shopping, you need to subtract the amount of money he spent from the amount of money he started with.

If he started with $100, and spent $60 on shoes and $12 on candy, you need to subtract: 100 – 60 – 12.

You could also add 60 + 12 first and then subtract that number from 100. However, Letter B is incorrect because the number sentence states that you add 60 + 12 and then subtract 100 more. This would give you an answer of -28. Students may select this answer choice if they are not looking carefully enough at the answer choices.

If you subtract 100 – 60 – 12, you will see that Joe has $28.00 left.

6. **D.** First, you need to determine how many people were invited to the party altogether. You do this by adding the number of people Rob invited, 22, to the number of people his mom invited, 3. 22 + 3 = 25 guests.

Next, you need to multiply 25 x 2 because each guest is going to have 2 cupcakes. 25 x 2 = 50.

7. **C, 37 points.** This question can be worth 2 points: 1 point for each correct answer.

To determine how many points The Dolphins scored altogether, you need to figure out how many points they scored in touchdowns, how many points they scored in field goals, and then add those two totals together.

$$7 \times 4 + 3 \times 3 = p$$

$$7 \times 4 = 28 \text{ and } 3 \times 3 = 9$$

$$28 + 9 = 37 \text{ points altogether}$$

8. **C, 274 pages.** This question can be worth 2 points: 1 point for each correct answer.

To determine how many pages Rachel has left to read, you first need to find out how many pages she has read so far. You can do this by multiplying the number of pages she read on Monday, Tuesday, and Wednesday 12, times the 3 days:

12 x 3 = 36. Next, you need to add this to the number of pages she read on Thursday, 15: 36 + 15 = 51 pages.

Last you need to subtract the total number of pages in the book and how many pages she has read so far: 325 – 51.

$$325 - 51 = 274 \text{ pages left}$$

9. **1st and 4th Choices, 21, $42.** To determine how many people are going to Muhammad's birthday, you need to first find out how many people were invited altogether: Muhammad invited 14 people and his mom invited 9: 14 + 9 = 23.

Next, you need to subtract 23 – 2 because 2 people cannot come to the party. 23 – 2 = 21.

Last, to determine the total cost of the goodie bags, you need to multiply the cost of each bag, $2, by the total number of goodie bags, 21: 21 x 2 = $42.00.

10. **Yes; Appropriate explanation.** Before you can determine whether or not Liz has enough money, you need to determine how much money she spent at the grocery store.

If she bought 2 bags of marshmallows and each bag costs $3, she spent $6.00 on marshmallows.

If she bought 2 boxes of crackers and each box costs $2, she spent $4 on crackers.

If she bought 10 candy bars and each candy bar costs $1, she spent $10 on candy bars.

Next, you need to add the total cost of each of these items together: $6 (marshmallows) + $4 (crackers) + $10 (candy bars) = $20.

If Liz plans to spend $20 at the grocery store, and she has $30 to spend, then she does have enough money. An appropriate student explanation will identify each step that needs to be solved before arriving at an answer. For example:

Yes, Liz has enough money. I know this because first I determined how much she plans to spend at the grocery store. I figured out that she would spend $6 on marshmallows because she wants to buy 2 bags for $2 each. I figured out that she would spend $4 on crackers because she wants to buy 2 bags for $2. I figured out that she would spend $10 on candy bars because she wants to buy 10 bars for $1 each. Then, I added each of these totals together: 6 + 4 + 10 = $20. If Liz has $30, she will have enough money because the items will only cost $20 altogether.

11. **50 cards, 40 cards, 15 more cards, 115 cards.** This question can be worth 4 points: 1 point for each correct answer.

First, you need to determine how many baseball cards Jake has. If Elle has 25 cards and Jake has twice as many, Jake has 50 cards: 25 x 2 = 50 cards

Next, you need to determine how many baseball cards Mark has. If Mark has 10 fewer baseball cards than Jake, Mark has 40 baseball cards: 50 – 10 = 40 cards

To determine how many more cards Jake has than Elle, you need to subtract the amount Jake has, 40, from the amount Elle has, 25: 40 – 25 = 15 more cards.

To determine how many baseball cards they have altogether, you add how many cards Elle has, 25, to how many cards Jake has, 50, to how many cards Mark has, 40.

$$25 + 50 + 40 = 115 \text{ cards altogether}$$

12. **180 miles, 50 days.** First, you need to determine how many miles Mrs. Winters ran in the first 10 days. If she ran 3 miles each day, then she ran 30 miles in the first 10 days because 3 x 10 = 30 miles.

Next, you need to determine how many miles Mrs. Winters ran in the second 10 days. If she ran 6 miles a day, then she ran 60 miles because 6 x 10 = 60 miles.

Then, you need to determine how many miles Mrs. Winters ran in the third 10 days. If she ran 9 miles a day, then she ran 90 miles because 9 x 10 = 90 miles.

To determine how many miles Mrs. Winters ran over the course of the 30 days, you add up the total number of days from each 10-day period: 30 + 60 + 90 = 180 miles.

To determine how many days it will take Mrs. Winters to run 15 miles, you will need to continue the pattern for each 10 day period: each 10 day period, she runs 3 more miles.

4th ten days: 12 miles
5th ten days: 15 miles

Mrs. Winters will be running 15 miles by the 5th ten-day period which means it will take her 50 days to run 15 miles.

3.OA.D.9. Identify & Understand Arithmetic Patterns

1. **C.** While it appears at first that this pattern is multiplying by 3, the pattern is actually adding by 3. 3 + 3 = 6 + 3 = 9 + 3 = 12 + 3 = 15

2. **A.** Letter *A* is an odd number because the last digit,

the digit in the ones place, is an odd number. Letters B, C, and D, are all even numbers because the last digit, the digit in the ones place, is an even number.

3. **C.** Letter C is correct because it only contains even numbers.

Letters A and B are incorrect because they only contain odd numbers. Letter D is incorrect because it contains both odd and even numbers.

4. **1st and 4th Choices.** 1st Choice is correct because 12 + 5 = 17, which is an odd number. 4th Choice D is correct because any odd number + an even number will always equal an odd number.

2nd Choice is incorrect because any odd number + any odd number will always equal an even number.

3rd Choice is incorrect because 7 + 7 = 14, which is an even number.

5. **D.** Letter D is correct because an even number + another even number will always equal another even number.

Letters B and C are incorrect because they are not ALWAYS true when adding an even number + an even number.

6. **See detailed explanation.** This question can be worth 4 points: 1 point for each correct answer in the table and 1 point for an appropriate explanation.

# of cars	3	4	5	6	7	8
# of wheels	12	16	**20**	24	**28**	32

Correct answers are in bold.

An appropriate student explanation will describe the rule for the pattern with evidence from the chart. For example, The rule for the chart is multiplying by 4. The total number of cars is multiplied by 4 to determine the total number of wheels. For example if there are 5 cars and each car has 4 wheels, there are 20 wheels altogether.

7. **D.** Letter D is correct because any even number + any odd number will always be an odd number.

Letters B and C are incorrect because they are not ALWAYS true.

8. **D.** Letter D is correct because each of the answers choices above are not ALWAYS true. Multiples of 5 can be odd or even and sometimes have a 5 in the ones place.

9. **Circle the 60; Appropriate explanation.** This question can be worth 2 points: 1 point for circling the number 60 and 1 point for an appropriate explanation.

An appropriate student explanation should refer to the rule of the numbers in the set and why the number 60 does not belong. For example: The number 60 does not belong because all of the numbers in the set are multiples of 9. For example, 9 x 1 = 9, 9 x 2 = 18, 9 x 4 = 36, 9 x 5 = 45, and 9 x 6 = 54. 60 is not a multiple of 9.

10. **See detailed explanation.** Students can agree or disagree with the statement as long as they can appropriately explain their thinking. However, if students have a strong understanding of patterns in the multiplication table, students should agree with the statement. An appropriate student explanation will describe this pattern. For example: I agree with Malik. I agree with Malik because if you know all of your 4s facts, all you have to do is double them to figure out your 8s facts. For example, if I know 4 x 2 = 8, I can figure out 8 x 2 because it will just be 4 x 2 doubled, which equals 16.

11. **See detailed explanation.** This question can be worth 9 points: 1 point for each appropriate explanation, and 1 point for correctly filling in each missing number in the multiplication table.

X	0	3	4	5	6	7
3	0	9	*12*	15	*18*	**21**
4	0	*12*	16	20	24	28
5	0	15	20	25	30	35
6	0	*18*	24	30	36	*42*
7	0	21	*28*	35	*42*	49

Numbers in italics are the correct answers for the missing numbers in the multiplication table.

Students may state that the student knows his zero facts or fives facts as long as they have an explanation that matches. For example:

This student knows his zero facts well. I know this because he filled in all of the zero facts on the multiplication chart, OR: This student knows his fives facts well. I know this because he filled in all of his fives facts horizontally and vertically in the multiplication table.

Students may state that the student still needs to practice his 3s facts, 4s facts, 6s facts, and 7s facts as long as they have an explanation that matches. For example: I know that this student still needs to practice his 3s facts because he didn't know 3 x 4 or 3 x 6, OR: I know that this student needs to practice his 4s facts because he didn't know 4 x 3 or 4 x 7.

12. **D, correct rule, yes; Appropriate**

explanation. The correct answer is D because this pattern is +3 − 5. Therefore, the next three digits in the sequence would be 22, 17, 20. The rule for the pattern is add 3 minus 5.

Yes, the number zero will never be a number in this pattern. I know this because if the pattern continues in +3 − 5, it would continue: 23, 18, 21, 16, 19, 14, 17, 12, 15, 10, 13, 8, 11, 6, 9, 4, 7, 2, 5, 0.

NUMBER AND OPERATIONS IN BASE TEN
3.NBT.1A.1. Round Whole Numbers

1. **B.** 34 rounded to the nearest 10 rounds down to 30. As the number line shows, 34 is closer to 30 than it is to 40. Also, the 4 in the ones place of 34 indicates that 34 needs to be rounded down to 30.

2. **D.** 256 rounded to the nearest 100 rounds up to 300. As the number line shows, 256 is closer to 300 than it is to 200. Also, the 5 in the tens place of 256 indicates that 256 needs to be rounded up to 300.

3.

Number	Round to the nearest 10	Round to the nearest 100
146	150	100
375	380	400
33	30	0
286	290	300

146 rounded to the nearest 10 rounds up to 150. The 6 in the ones place of 146 indicates that it rounds up to 150.

146 rounded to the nearest 100 rounds down to 100. The 4 in the tens place of 146 indicates that it rounds down to 100.

375 rounded to the nearest 10 rounds up to 380. The 5 in the ones place of 375 indicates that it rounds up to 380.

375 rounded to the nearest 100 rounds up to 400. The 7 in the tens place of 375 indicates that it rounds up to 400.

33 rounded to the nearest 10 rounds down to 30. The 3 in the ones place of 33 indicates that it rounds down to 30.

33 rounded to the nearest 100 rounds down to 0. The 3 in the tens place of 33 indicates that it rounds down to 0.

286 rounded to the nearest 10 rounds up to 290. The 6 in the ones place of 286 indicates that the number rounds up to 290.

286 rounded to the nearest 100 rounds up to 300. The 8 in the tens place of 286 indicates that the number rounds up to 300.

4. **1st, 2nd, 5th Choices,** 50 rounds to 100 because the 5 in the tens place of 50 indicates that the number rounds up to 100.

125 rounds to 100 because the 2 in the tens place of 125 indicates that the number rounds down to 100.

150 rounds to 200 because the 5 in the tens place of 150 indicates that the number rounds up to 200.

45 rounds to 0 because the 4 in the tens place of 45 indicates that the number rounds down to 0.

85 rounds to 100 because the 8 in the tens place of 85 indicates that the number rounds up to 100.

5. **D.** 17 rounded to the nearest 10 rounds up to 20. The 7 in the ones place of 17 indicates that the number rounds up to 20.

6. **B.** 1,056 rounded to the nearest 100 rounds up to 1,100. The 5 in the tens place of 1,056 indicates that the number rounds up to 1,100.

Choice a is incorrect because it rounds 1,056 to the nearest 1,000.

Choice d is incorrect because it rounds 1,056 to the nearest 10.

7. **C.** When rounding to the nearest 10, 15 does NOT round to 10. The 5 in the ones place indicates that the number rounds up to 20.

5 rounds up to 10 because the 5 in the ones place indicates that the number rounds up.

11 rounds down to 10 because the 1 in the ones place indicates that the number rounds down.

13 rounds down to 10 because the 3 in the ones place indicates that the number rounds down.

8. **Emily is incorrect.** This question can be worth 2 points: 1 point for having the correct answer, Emily is incorrect, and 1 point having a specific explanation. An appropriate explanation should explain why Emily is incorrect AND how to correctly round 150 to the nearest 100. When rounding to the nearest 100, 150 does not round down to 100. For example, Emily is incorrect. Emily is incorrect because when you are rounding to the nearest 100, 150 does not round down. When rounding to the nearest 100, 150 rounds up to 200. The 5 in the tens place tells us to round up to the next nearest 100.

9. **C.** Choice C is correct because it rounds each number to the nearest 10 to find the sum. 235 rounded to the nearest 10 rounds to 240 and 452 rounded to the nearest 10 rounds to 450. 240 + 450 = 690.

Choice B is incorrect because it rounds each number to the nearest 100 to find the sum.

10. **A.** 34 rounded to the nearest 10 rounds down to

30. You need to add 30 + 30 because each guest is going to have approximately 2 cookies. 30 + 30 = 60 cookies.

The clue word 'about' tells us that we are rounding or finding an estimate.

11. This question can be worth 3 points: 1 point for a correct answer to part one, 1 point for a correct answer to part two, and 1 point for a specific explanation in part two.

There are a variety of different answer choices, depending on if students round to the nearest 10 or to the nearest 100.

Rounding to the nearest 10: 117 rounds up to 120, 87 rounds up to 90, and 104 rounds to 100.

$$120 + 90 + 100 = 310$$

Rounding to the nearest 100: 117 rounds down to 100, 87 rounds up to 100, and 104 rounds down to 100.

$$100 + 100 + 100 = 300$$

For the next part, student answers will again depending on whether they have rounded the first part to the nearest 10 or the nearest 100.

Rounding to the nearest 10: First, students should round 42 down to 40. Next, students should add 40 to the 310 they found in the first part. 310 + 40 = 350. When rounding to the nearest 10, Nick is correct. An example of an appropriate explanation is: Nick is correct. I know this because Chris got about 40 new sports cards for his birthday. He already had about 310 sports cards.

$$310 + 40 = 350 \text{ sports cards.}$$

Rounding to the nearest 100: In this case, students may choose to round the 42 to the nearest 10, which would be 40, or the students may choose to round 42 to the nearest 100, which would be 0.

Rounding 42 to the nearest 10: If students rounded 40 to the nearest 10, they would add 300 + 40 = 340. Depending on students choose to explain their answer, Nick could be correct or incorrect.

Possible explanation 1: Nick is correct. I know this because Chris got about 40 new sports cards for his birthday. He already had about 300 sports cards. 300 + 40 = 340. Nick is correct because 340 is only 10 away from 350.

Possible explanation 2: Nick is incorrect. I know this because Chris got about 40 new sports cards for his birthday. He already had about 300 sports cards. 300 + 40 = 340. 340 rounded to the nearest 10 is 340, and 340 rounded to the nearest 100 is 300. Therefore, Nick is incorrect.

Rounding 42 to the nearest 100: If students rounded 40 to the nearest 100, they would add 300 + 0 = 300. When rounding to the nearest 100, Nick is incorrect. An example of an appropriate explanation is: Nick is incorrect. I know this because Nick got 42 sports cards for his birthday. 42 rounded to the nearest 100 is 0. He already had about 300 sports cards. 300 + 0 = 300. Therefore, Nick is incorrect.

12. **D.** First, students need to determine about how much money Shawn spent by rounding his purchases to the nearest dollar.

$$\$4.50 \text{ rounds to } \$5.00$$
$$\$6.76 \text{ rounds to } \$7.00$$
$$\$15.99 \text{ rounds to } \$16.00$$

Next, students will add these amounts together to determine about how much money Shawn spent.

$$\$5.00 + \$7.00 + \$16.00 = \$28.00.$$

Students may then choose to round $28.00 to the nearest ten dollars which is $30.00. This would make for easy mental subtraction of $50.00 - $30.00 = $20.00

Students may also choose to keep the $28.00. In this case, $50.00 - $28.00 = $22.00. If students choose to solve the problem this way, they will see that there is no answer choice of $22.00. This will force them to go back and solve the problem again.

Choice C is incorrect because this is the actual amount of money that Shawn spent. The clue word 'about' indicates that you should round or estimate to find your answer.

3.NBT.A.2. Add & Subtract Whole Numbers

1. **D.** When you write a number in expanded form, it means you expand the number to show the value of each digit. For example, 127 = 100 + 20 + 7

2. **C.** When you write a number in standard form, you are writing the number as it is typically seen. It is the opposite of expanded form.

$$\text{For example, } 500 + 30 + 9 = 539$$

3. **A.** 50
   + 45 = 50 + 40 + 5 = 95

4. **C.** 417
   − 203 = 400 − 200 = 200, 10 − 0 = 10,
   7 − 3 = 4
   200 + 10 + 4 = 214

5. **2nd, 3rd, 4th Choices.** This question can be worth 3 points: 1 point for each correct answer.

$$50 - 35 = 50 - 30 - 5 = 15$$

$$30 - 15 = 30 - 10 - 5 = 15$$
$$45 - 30 = 40 - 30 - 5 = 15$$
$$15 - 0 = 15$$

6. **1,010.**
$392 + 618 = N$
$300 + 600 = 900$
$90 + 10 = 100$
$2 + 8 = 10$
$1,010$

7. **D; 884 pumpkin seeds.** This question can be worth 2 points: 1 point for each correct answer.

The clue word "altogether" indicates that you need to add the total number of seeds Jon has, 485 seeds, and the total number of seeds Claire has, 549 seeds.

$$485 + 549 = N.$$

To determine how many seeds were left after Jon and Claire's mom used 150 seeds, you need to subtract 150 seeds from the total number of seeds.

$485 + 549 = 400 + 500 = 900, 80 + 40 = 120,$
$$9 + 5 = 14$$
$900 + 120 + 14 = 1,034$ total seeds
$1,034 - 150 = 884$ pumpkin seeds left

8. **C.** $135 - 50 = 130 - 50 = 80 + 5 = 85$

9. **Appropriate explanation; D.** The mistake that Ana made is that she did kept her 10 ones instead of making them into one 10.

$$300 + 600 = 900$$
$$50 + 10 = 60$$
$$4 + 6 = 10$$
$$900 + 60 + 10 = 970$$
So $354 + 616 = 970.$

10. **1st and 2nd Choices; 532 stickers.** This question can be worth 3 points: 1 point for each correct answer.

To determine how many stickers Sam has altogether, you need to add how many he starts with, 293, to the amounts he gets from his friends: 150 from Abby and 89 from Helen.

$293 + 150 + 89 = 532$ stickers altogether.

2nd Choice is also correct because $150 + 89 = 239$. So: $293 + 239 = 532$ stickers.

11. **No.** This question can be worth 2 points: 1 point for the correct answer and 1 point for an appropriate explanation.

Using mental math and estimation, students will determine that Luke does not have enough money. An appropriate explanation describes how estimation and/or mental math was used. For example:

No, Luke does not have enough money. I know this because first I rounded the cost of the video game, $19.99, to the nearest dollar: $20.00. Then I rounded the cost of the book, $14.99, to the nearest dollar $15.00. Then I rounded the cost of the shirt, $19.99, to the nearest dollar, $20.00.

After that, I added the 3 rounded amounts together:

$20 + $15 + $20 = $55. If Luke only has $50, he will not have enough money.

12. **False.** This question can be worth 2 points: 1 point for the correct answer and 1 point for an appropriate explanation.

1,000 − 439 does not have a difference less than 500.

An appropriate explanation will specifically describe how to solve the problem with a clear understanding of place value. For example:

I would tell Charlie that he should always start subtracting in the ones place. If you don't have any ones that you can subtract, see if you can borrow a ten. If you can't borrow a ten, see if you can borrow a hundred. If you can't borrow a hundred, see if you can borrow a thousand. Take 1,000 and break it down into 10 hundreds. Then you can give 1 of your hundreds to the 10s and you can give 1 of your 10s to your 1s. $10 - 9 = 1$. So we have 1 one. Next, we can subtract the 9 tens we have left from 30. $90 - 30 = 60$. Then, we can subtract the 9 hundreds we have left from 400. $900 - 400 = 500$. We do not have any thousands left. So, $1,000 - 439 = 500 + 60 + 1 = 561$.

If students choose, they may also draw an illustration of base-10 blocks to show how to solve this problem.

3.NBT.A.3. Multiply Multiples of 10

1. **C.** $5 \times 10 = 50$

$10 + 10 + 10 + 10 + 10 = 50$

2. **D.** $10 \times 10 = 100$

$10 + 10 + 10 + 10 + 10 + 10 + 10 + 10 + 10 + 10 = 100$

3. **A.** $2 \times 20 = 40$

The product of 2×20 is the same as the fact in the tens place ($2 \times 2 = 4$) and a zero in the ones place.

4. **1st, 2nd & 4th Choices.** $3 \times 40 = 120$

The product of 3×40 is the same as the fact in the tens place ($3 \times 4 = 12$) and a zero in the ones place.

120 is an even number and is greater than 100.

5. **1st, 2nd and 4th Choices.** $4 \times 50 = 200$

The product of 4×50 is the same as the fact in the tens place ($4 \times 5 = 20$) and a zero in the ones place.

$50 + 50 + 50 + 50$ also equals 200.

20 x 10 = 200

50 x 4 equals 200.

6. **C; yes;** This question measures a student's ability to apply multiplying by multiples of 10 in a word problem.

10 x what number equals 45? Students will see that this does not equal a whole number. Therefore, the options are 10 x 4 = 40 or 10 x 5 = 50. The correct answer is 5 weeks because if Alex only saved for 4 weeks, he would only have earned $40. This means that Alex will have money left over. An appropriate explanation states why.

Yes, Alex will have money left over. Alex will have $5.00 left over because he needs to save up for 5 weeks. If he earns $10 a week and saves for 5 weeks, he will have earned $50. If the bat costs $45, he will have $5 left over.

7. **A.** To determine how much it will cost the third grade to go on the field trip, you must first determine the total cost of the bus. To determine the total cost of the bus, you multiply the number of students, 20, by the cost per student, $3.

20 x $3 = $60 for the bus.

Next, you need to determine the total cost of the admission tickets. To determine the total cost of admission, you multiply the number of students, 20, by the cost per student, $4. 20 x $4 = $80 for admission.

Last, you add the total cost of the bus and the total cost of admission together: $60 + $80 = $140.

8. This question can be worth 6 points: 1 point for each correct answer in the chart and 1 point for identifying the correct rule.

INPUT	2	3	4	5	6	7
OUTPUT	160	240	*320*	400	*480*	560

Correct answers in the chart are written in italics.

The rule for the table is multiplying the input number by 80.

2 x 80 = 160, 3 x 8 = 240, 4 x 8 = 320, 5 x 8 = 400, 6 x 8 = 480, 7 x 8 = 560

9. **3rd and 4th Choices.** This question can be worth 2 points: 1 point for each correct answer.

1st and 2nd choices are incorrect because:
20 x 5 = 100 and 6 x 30 = 180

3rd and 4th choices are correct because:
4 x 60 = 240 and 30 x 7 = 210.

10. **B.** An appropriate explanation links multiplying by multiples of 10 to multiplying basic facts. For example:

Mike can use 8 x 6 to help him solve 80 x 6 because all he has to do is solve 8 x 6 and add a zero in the ones place. 8 x 6 = 48. With a zero in the ones place, 80 x 6 = 480.

11. **False, True, True, False, True.** This question can be worth 7 points: 1 point for each correct answer and 1 point for each correct equation for the false statements.

30 x 100 = 300 is false. 30 x 100 = 3,000
50 x 4 = 200 is true.
240 ÷ 80 = 3 is true.
1,000 ÷ 50 = 5 is false. 1,000 ÷ 50 = 20
20 x 800 = 1600 is true.

12. **$20; $80; $140.** This question can be worth 3 points: 1 point for each correct answer

To determine how much money Dan has, you need to divide the amount of money Kevin has, $40, by 2 because Kevin has 2 times the amount of money that Dan has: $40 ÷ 2 = $20. Dan has $20.

To determine how much money Lauren has, you need to multiply the amount of money Dan has, $20, by 4 because Lauren has 4 times the amount of money that Dan has.

$20 x 4 = $80. Lauren has $80.

To determine how much money they have altogether, you need to add how money they each have: $40 + $20 + $80 = $140

NUMBER & OPERATIONS – FRACTIONS
3.NF.A.1. Identify & Understand Fractions

1. **A.** The rectangle has 4 parts. Each part is worth $1/4$. Only 1 part is shaded, so the answer is $1/4$.

2. **C.** This circle is divided into 6 parts. Each part is worth $1/6$. Two parts are shaded, so the answer is $2/6$.

3. **$4/6$.** The rectangle has 6 parts. Each part is worth $1/6$. Four parts are shaded, so the fraction is $4/6$.

4. This question can be worth 2 points: 1 point for the correct answer and 1 point for the correct explanations.

To show the fraction $2/8$, students should have shaded in 2 hearts. Since there are eight parts, each part is worth $1/8$.

Students should state that the numerator tells how many parts are being counted or shaded, while the denominator tells how many parts there are altogether. Specifically, to these figures, the numerator tells that 2 parts are shaded and the denominator tells that there are 8 parts altogether.

5. This question demonstrates a student's understanding that fractions relate to equal parts. Therefore, they should have circled the rectangles and

the circle. The triangle and parallelogram are divided into 6 parts, but each part is not equal.

6. **D; C.** This question can be worth 2 points: 1 point for each correct answer.

The apple pie is divided into 8 parts. Each part is worth $\frac{1}{8}$. Chris eats two parts, so he eats $\frac{2}{8}$ of the apple pie.

If Chris eats 2 slices, that means there are four slices, our four parts left. Therefore, the fraction of the pie that is left is $\frac{4}{6}$.

7. **2nd and 3rd Choices.** This question can be worth 2 points: 1 point for each correct answer.

The rectangle is divided into 6 equal parts. Each part is worth $\frac{1}{6}$. 3 parts are shaded. Therefore, $\frac{3}{6}$ or $\frac{1}{2}$ of the figure is shaded. 1st and 4th Choices are not correct because the fractions are equivalent to whole numbers.

8. **B.** A pizza has 12 slices. Each slice is worth $\frac{1}{12}$ If 4 slices are pepperoni and 3 slices are sausage, that takes 7 slices of the pizza. If you subtract 7 from 12, you see that there are 5 pieces or $\frac{5}{12}$ of the pizza left.

9. **1st and 3rd Choices.** This question can be worth 2 points: 1 point for each correct answer.

There are 6 blocks. Each block is worth $\frac{1}{6}$. 2 blocks are red and 1 block is black, so that takes 3 blocks. If you subtract 3 from 6, you see that there are 3 yellow blocks left. This can be represented as $\frac{3}{6}$ or $\frac{1}{2}$.

10. **2nd and 3rd Choices; 2nd and 4th Choices.** This question can be worth 4 points: 1 point for each correct answer.

If 3 friends are sharing 4 brownies, they can split them up in a variety of ways. If they split each brownie up into 3 slices, then there would be 12 slices in all, or $\frac{12}{3}$. Each friend would get $\frac{4}{3}$. Twelve divided by three = four slices, or $\frac{4}{3}$.

If each person got 1 whole brownie, then there would be 1 whole brownie left. This brownie could then be split into thirds, and each person would get one-third of the last brownie. This correlates to 1 $\frac{1}{3}$ brownies per person.

If the brownies were split into 4 pieces, that would create a total of 16 pieces altogether. You cannot equally divide 16 slices of brownies among 3 people.

11. **D; $18.** This question can be worth 2 points: 1 point for each correct answer.

To determine $\frac{1}{4}$ of $24, you divide 4 into 24. Since 24 ÷ 4 = 6, this means that Dan spent $6. To determine how much money Dan had left, you subtract 6 from 24, which equals $18.

12. **B; B.** This question can be worth 2 points: 1 point for each correct answer.

If there are 40 treats, and $\frac{1}{2}$ were sold in the morning and $\frac{1}{4}$ were sold in the afternoon, this means that there is still $\frac{1}{4}$ left. This is true because $\frac{1}{2} + \frac{1}{4} + \frac{1}{4}$ = one whole.

If there are 40 treats, and $\frac{1}{2}$ were sold in the morning, then that means 20 treats were sold in the morning. If $\frac{1}{4}$ of the treats were sold in the afternoon, then that means that 10 treats were sold in the afternoon. To determine how many treats were left, you subtract:

40 − 20 − 10 = 10 treats left.

3.NF.A.2. Represent & Understand Fractions on a Number Line

1. **C.** This number line starts at 0, ends at 1, and is divided into 3 equal parts. The mark is on the second part, signifying the fraction $\frac{2}{3}$.

2. **A.** This number line starts at 0, ends at 1, and is divided into 6 equal parts. The mark is on the second part, signifying the fraction $\frac{2}{6}$.

3. The number line starts at 0, ends at 1, and is divided into 8 equal parts. To show the fraction $\frac{5}{8}$, students must draw a mark on the 5th part or the 5th tick mark.

4. **A and C Choices.** This question can be worth 2 points: 1 point for each correct answer.

This number line starts at 0, ends at 1, and is divided into 4 equal parts. The mark is on the second part, signifying the fraction $\frac{2}{4}$. The number line can also be seen is divided into 2 equal parts. In this case, the mark is on the first part, signifying the fraction $\frac{1}{2}$.

Students should recognize that the fractions $\frac{2}{4}$ and $\frac{1}{2}$ are equivalent.

5. **A.** There are three thirds in one whole because

$\frac{1}{3} + \frac{1}{3} + \frac{1}{3} = \frac{3}{3}$ or 1 whole.

6. This question can be worth 2 points: 1 point for correctly drawing the number line and 1 point for correctly labeling the fraction.

Students should divide the number line into 6 equal parts. Students should then draw a mark over the 5th part or tick mark, representing the fraction $\frac{5}{6}$.

7. **D.** This number line starts at 0, ends at 1, and is divided into 8 equal parts. Any fraction with a denominator that is a factor of 8 could appear on this number line. 2, 8, and 4 are all factors of 8.

The fraction $\frac{1}{3}$ would not appear on the number line because 8 is not divisible by 3.

8. **2nd and 3rd Choices.** This question can be worth 2 points: 1 point for each correct answer.

Students should select the 2nd and 3rd answer choices. The 2nd number line starts at 0, ends at 1, and is divided into 3 equal parts. $1/3$ would be placed on the first tick mark. The 3rd number line starts at 0, ends at 1, and is divided into 6 equal parts. $1/3$ would be placed on the second tick mark because $1/3$ and $2/6$ are equivalent fractions.

The first number line is divided into 5 equal parts. Since the denominator in $1/3$ is not divisible by 5, the fraction would not appear on this number line.

The fourth number line is divided into 4 equal parts. Since the denominator in $1/3$ is not divisible by 4, the fraction would not appear on this number line.

9. **D; See detailed explanation.** This question can be worth 3 points: 1 point for the correct answer, 1 point for an accurately drawn number line diagram, and 1 point for an appropriate explanation.

$1/4$ and $3/4$ are $2/4$ apart.

Students should draw a number line that starts at 0, ends at 1, and is divided into 4 equal parts. The fractions $1/4$ and $3/4$ should be labeled on the number line. Students should draw 2 jumps from $1/4$ to $3/4$ to show that the fractions are $2/4$ a part.

An appropriate student explanation may state: I know that the fractions $1/4$ and $3/4$ are $2/4$ apart. I know this because it takes 2 jumps that are worth $1/4$ each to get from $1/4$ to $3/4$.

10. **A and C Choices.** This question can be worth 3 points: 1 point for each correct answer and 1 point for an appropriate explanation.

This number line starts at 0 and ends at 4. The mark is above the 2nd tick mark, or the whole number 2. This can be represented as $2/1$ or as $4/2$.

The fractions $0/2$ and $2/4$ don't work because they equal less than one whole.

An appropriate student explanation may state: No, I do not agree with Darnell. I do not agree with Darnell because $4/2$ is a fraction that represents 2 wholes. This number line is divided into 4 wholes and the mark is on the 2nd whole. Therefore, $4/2$ does fit on this number line.

11. **D; See detailed explanation.** This question can be worth 3 points: 1 point for the correct answer, 1 point for an accurate picture, and 1 point for an appropriate explanation.

The carpenter will need 2 pieces of wood. If he needs $12/8$ of wood, then each piece of wood is divided into 8 parts. With the numerator greater than 8, we know that he will need another piece of wood. He won't need 3 pieces of wood unless he needs $24/8$.

An appropriate student drawing may show 2 rectangles, each rectangle cut into 8 equal parts. In the first rectangle, all parts would be shaded to represent 1 whole or $8/8$. In the second rectangle, 4 parts would be shaded to represent the addition 4 parts needed to make 12.

An appropriate student explanation may state: I know that the carpenter will need 2 pieces of wood. I know this because he needs $12/8$ of wood. When the numerator is bigger than the denominator, this means you have more than one whole. This means the carpenter will need an entire piece of wood and 4 pieces of another piece of wood to make 12 pieces altogether. If each piece of wood is cut into 8 pieces, that equals a total of $12/8$ of wood.

12. **See detailed explanation.** The first number line starts at 0, ends at 1, and is divided into 3 equal parts. Therefore, this number line can represent the fractions: $1/3$ and $2/3$.

The second number line starts at 0, ends at 4, and is divided into 4 equal parts. Therefore, this number line can represent the fractions : $6/2$ and $6/6$. These are the only fractions that represent whole numbers between 0 and 4.

The third number line starts at 0, ends at 1, and is divided into 6 equal parts. Therefore, this number line can represent the fractions: $1/3$, $4/6$, $6/6$, and $2/3$. The fraction $1/3$ should be labeled on the second tick mark. The fractions $4/6$ and $2/3$ should be labeled on the fourth tick mark. The fraction $6/6$ should be labeled on the last tick mark, the 1.

The fractions that appear on more than one number line are: $1/3$ and $2/3$.

An appropriate student explanation may state: The fraction $1/3$ appears on the first number line and the third number line. This is possible because $1/3$ and $2/6$ are equivalent fractions. I know this because they are on the same spot on the number line.

3.NF.A.3. Compare Fractions

1. **C.** This question is comparing fractions with the same denominator. When comparing fractions with the same denominator, the fraction with the bigger numerator is the greater fraction.

In this case, $2/8 < 5/8$.

2. **A.** This question is comparing fractions with the same numerator. When comparing fractions with the same numerator, the fraction with the smaller denominator is the greater fraction.

In this case, $1/4 < 1/2$.

3. **B.** This question identifies equivalent fractions. When the numerator and the denominator are the same, it

equals one whole.

In this case, $^6/_6 = ^1/_1$.

4. 2nd, 3rd and 5th Choices. This question can be worth 3 points: 1 point for each correct answer.

Students should have selected the 2nd, 3rd, and 5th answer choices. Any fractions that are greater than 0 and less than 1 will fit on a number line between 0 and 1. $^1/_2$, $^1/_9$, and $^3/_4$ are each less than one whole.

5. A; Appropriate explanation. This question can be worth 2 points: 1 point for the correct answers and 1 point for an appropriate explanation.

The fraction $^5/_5$ is equal to one whole because the numerator and denominator are the same.

An appropriate student explanation may state: I know that $^5/_5$ is equal to one whole. There are 5 equal parts and all 5 parts are taken away. Students may also draw an illustration that shows a figure with 5 equal parts and all 5 parts shaded.

6. Hillary; Appropriate explanation and picture. This question can be worth 3 points: 1 point for the correct answer, 1 point for an appropriate explanation, and 1 point for an appropriate picture.

Hillary is correct because the fractions $^2/_4$ and $^4/_8$ are equivalent. If both girls had the same size sundae, then they both ate half of their large sundae.

An appropriate student explanation may state: Hillary is correct. I know this because the fractions $^2/_4$ and $^4/_8$ mean the same thing. They are both equal to $^1/_2$ which means both girls ate half of their ice cream sundaes.

Students should draw an illustration that shows that $^2/_4$ and $^4/_8$ represent the same amount.

7. C. This number line starts at 0 and ends at 2. Letter C is situated at one whole. The fraction $^2/_2$ represents one whole because the numerator and denominator are the same.

8. 1st, 3rd and 5th Choices. This question can be worth 3 points: 1 point for each correct answer.

Students should have selected the 1st, 3rd, and 5th answer choices. Letter B is situated halfway between the 0 tick mark and the 1 whole tick mark. This number line is divided into halves, fourths, and eighths. Therefore, the fractions $^1/_2$, $^2/_4$ and $^4/_8$ can all be represented by Letter B.

9. See detailed explanation. This question can be worth 2 points: 1 point for an appropriate explanation and 1 point for an appropriate drawing.

This question measures a student's understanding of the size of a whole. The reason that Wally ate more pizza than Elijah is because his whole was larger than Elijah's. An appropriate student explanation may state: It is possible that Wally ate more pizza than Elijah because his pizza was bigger.

Students should draw an illustration that shows Elijah eating $^1/_2$ of a small pizza and Wally eating $^1/_4$ of a much larger pizza.

10. 2nd and 5th Choices. Students should have selected the 2nd and 5th answer choices.

The 1st and 3rd answer choice shows fractions in order from greatest to least. The 4th answer choice shows all equivalent fractions.

11. See detailed explanation. This question can be worth 3 points: 2 points for drawing each fraction correctly on the number line and 1 point for an appropriate explanation.

Student number lines should look like the example below:

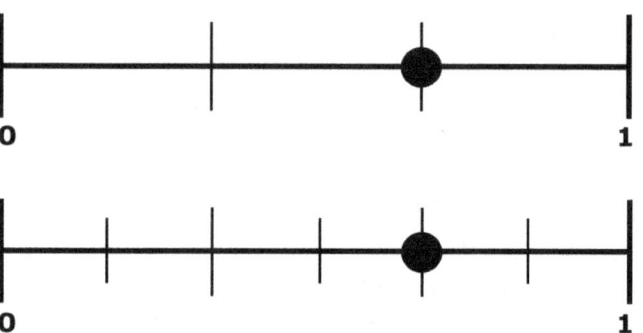

An appropriate student explanation may state: I know that the fractions $^2/_3$ and $^4/_5$ are equivalent. I know this because they represent the same point on the number line.

12. Abbey; Appropriate explanation; D; Appropriate explanation. This question can be worth 4 points: 1 point for each correct answer and 1 point for each appropriate explanation.

If Abbey ate one slice of pie from Mrs. Clark's pie, and Mrs. Clark's pie was split up into 4 slices, then Abbey ate $^1/_4$ of the pie.

If Jessica ate two slices of pie from Mrs. Shelton's pie, and Mrs. Shelton's pie was split up into 12 slices, then Jessica ate $^2/_{12}$ of the pie.

Abbey ate more pie because $^1/_4 > ^2/_{12}$. We can determine this by reducing the fraction $^2/_{12}$ into $^1/_6$.

$^1/_6 < ^1/_4$ because the slice of pie would be smaller.

An appropriate student explanation may state: Abbey ate more pie. I know this because $^1/_4 > ^2/_{12}$. Even though Abbey ate one slice of pie, her slice was bigger than both of Jessica's slices.

In order for both girls to eat the same amount of pie, Abbey would have to eat $^1/_4$ and Jessica would have to eat $3/_{12}$.

An appropriate student explanation my state: I know that if Abbey ate $1/_4$ of the pie and Jessica ate $3/_{12}$ of the pie, they would eat the same amount. I know this because $1/_4$ and $3/_{12}$ are equivalent fractions.

*Higher level students may explain how they simplified the fraction $3/_{12}$ to determine that it was equal to $1/_4$.

*Other students may determine the fractions are equal by drawing a number line or picture.

MEASUREMENT AND DATA
3.MD.A.1. Tell Time & Solve Word Problems Involving Time Intervals

1. **C.** This clock shows the time 3:37. The hour hand is between the hours of 3 and 4. The minute hand is 2 minutes past the 7, which signifies 35 minutes. Therefore, the time is 3:37.

2. **A.** This clock shows 10:29. The hour hand is just about between the hours of 10 and 11. The minute hand is 4 minutes past the 5, which signifies 25 minutes. Therefore, the time is 10:29.

3. **1st and 5th Choices.** The time between 6.30 and 7.00 is 30 minutes. 30 minutes is the same amount of time as a half hour.

4. **B.** The point on the number line shows the time 5:10. The number line is divided into 10-minute increments. Therefore, the first tick mark after 5:00 would represent 5:10.

5. **D.** This clock shows 3:07. The hour hand is slightly past the 3. The minute hand is 2 minutes past the 5, which signifies 5 minutes. Therefore, the time is 3:07.

6. **See detailed explanation.** It is 3:07. In 8 minutes, it will be 3:15.

Students should draw this time on the clock by showing the hour hand a little past the hour hand of the 3, but not quite halfway between the 3 and the 4. The minute hand should be directly on the 3, signifying 15 minutes.

7. **B.** If Chris started his chores at 7:15, and it took him 35 minutes to do his chores, then he finished his chores at 7:50. Number line B has the point on the time 7:50.

8. **1st and 3rd Choices.** This question can be worth 2 points: 1 point for each correct answer.

Clock A shows the time 11:48. Clock B shows the time 1:21. This means that 1 hour and 33 minutes passes between the two clocks.

The 1st and 3rd answer choices represent the time of 1 hour and 33 minutes.

The 3rd answer choice represents the time elapsed in just minutes: 93 minutes.

9. **Elementary School Musical, Little Lego Monsters;** This question can be worth 2 points: 1 point for each correct answer.

Fish and Sharks and Whales, Oh My! is 1 hour and 25 minutes long.

Elementary School Musical is 1 hour and 35 minutes long.

Little Lego Monsters is 1 hour and 10 minutes long.

The longest movie is *Elementary School Musical*.

If Chad can only see a movie that is 1 hour and 15 minutes long, then he can see *Little Lego Monsters*. The other two movies are too long.

10. **D; A.** This question can be worth 2 points: 1 point for each correct answer.

In order to determine how long it takes Betty to get ready, you simply add the amount of time it takes her to do each task: 10 minutes (shower), 5 minutes (get dressed), 15 minutes (eat), and 7 minutes (gather materials.)

$$10 + 5 + 15 + 7 = 37 \text{ minutes.}$$

In order to determine what time Betty will be ready for school, you simply add the amount of minutes it takes her to get ready to the time she begins getting ready: 6:15.

$$6:15 + 37 \text{ minutes} = 6:52$$

11. **C.** In order to determine the correct number line, students need to first determine the scale for each number line.

The first number line doesn't make sense because 6:45 and 7:15 are right next to each other.

The second number and fourth number lines don't make sense because you cannot count from 6:45 to 7:15 on this number line based on the tick marks shown.

The third number line shows a scale of counting by 10 minutes intervals between tick marks and correctly places the time of 7:15.

12. **B, 6:30.** This question can be worth 2 points: 1 point for each correct answer.

In order to determine what time Oliver started his chores, you first need to determine how long it took him to do his chores. You can find this out by adding the amount of time it took him to complete each task. 35 minutes (homework) + 13 minutes (shower) + 6 minutes (make lunch) + 12 minutes (fold laundry).

$$35 + 13 + 6 + 12 = 66 \text{ minutes.}$$

Once you know how long it took Oliver to complete his

chores, you can subtract this from the time he finished his chores: 8:00.

$$8:00 - 66 \text{ minutes} = 6:54.$$

In order to determine what time dinner started, you subtract the amount of time dinner lasted, 24 minutes, from the time he started his chores: 6:54.

$$6:54 - 24 \text{ minutes} = 6:30.$$

MD.A.2. Estimate & Measure Liquid Volume & Mass

1. **A.** Grams are used to measure the mass of small, lightweight objects, similar to a paper clip. 1 paper clip typically has a mass of about 1 gram. 100 grams, 1 kilogram, and 10 kilograms are too large of measurements for the mass of a pencil.

2. **C.** Capacity is another word for volume. One drop of liquid from a typical eyedropper measures about 1 milliliter. The liquid in 1 typical bottle of soda measures about 2 liters. 10 liters is too large for the capacity of the pitcher. 10 milliliters and 2 milliliters are too small for the capacity of the pitcher.

3. **Cell phone: less than 1 kg; Paper airplane: less than 1 kg; Grand piano: more than 1 kg.** Kilograms are used to measure the mass of large, heavy objects, similar to a bag of rice.

4. **C.** Choices A and B are not possible because these units are used to measure liquid volume.

Choice D is not possible because 5 grams is too small to be the mass of a toaster.

5. **B.** Choices C and D are not possible because these units are used to measure mass.

Choice A is not possible because 20 liters is too much to be the capacity of a pitcher of lemonade.

6. **A bunch of bananas; a pineapple.** A dishwasher, an oven and a refrigerator have a mass much greater than 1 kilogram.

7. **Student correctly shades the container of milk to the bolded line that states 2L; Student correctly shades the container of cream to the bolded line that states 1L; Steve needs 1 more liter of milk than cream; Steve needs 3 liters of milk and cream altogether; Steve will need 6 liters of milk and cream altogether when he doubles the recipe.** This can be a 5 point question: 1 point for correctly shading the milk container, 1 point for correctly shading the cream container, 1 point for the correct computations of how much more milk than cream, how much cream and milk altogether, and how much cream and milk altogether when the recipe is doubled.

Steve needs 2 liters of milk and 1 liter of cream.

2 liters of milk minus 1 liter of cream = Steve needs 1 more liter of milk than cream.

2 liters of milk plus 1 liter of cream = 3 liters of milk and cream altogether.

3 liters of milk and cream altogether for one recipe

This needs to be doubled or multiplied by 2 when making 2 cakes. $3 \times 2 = 6$ liters of milk and cream altogether.

8. **D.** One bucket of water = 4 liters

If Nyasia needs 28 liters of water altogether, you need to divide $28 \div 4 = 7$.

Nyasia will need to fill the bucket 7 times until the tank is full.

9. **Total mass of Harper's luggage = 40 kilograms; Harper will need to pay \$125.** This can be worth 3 points: 1 point for the correct total mass of Harper's luggage, 1 point for the correct cost of Harper's luggage, and 1 point for showing work using pictures, numbers, or words.

The clue words *total mass* indicate that you need to add 25 kilograms + 15 kilograms = 40 kilograms.

Harper has 40 total kilograms of luggage. If the first 15 kilograms of luggage are free, you need to determine the total mass of the luggage Harper will need to pay for. $40 - 15 = 25$ kilograms.

Each kilogram then costs \$5. You need to multiply the total number of kilograms Harper will have to pay for and the cost per kilogram to determine the total cost she needs to pay. $25 \times 5 = \$125$

Appropriate pictorial representations may include drawings illustrating the luggage's mass as well as cost. Student will likely include equations to show math as well. For example:

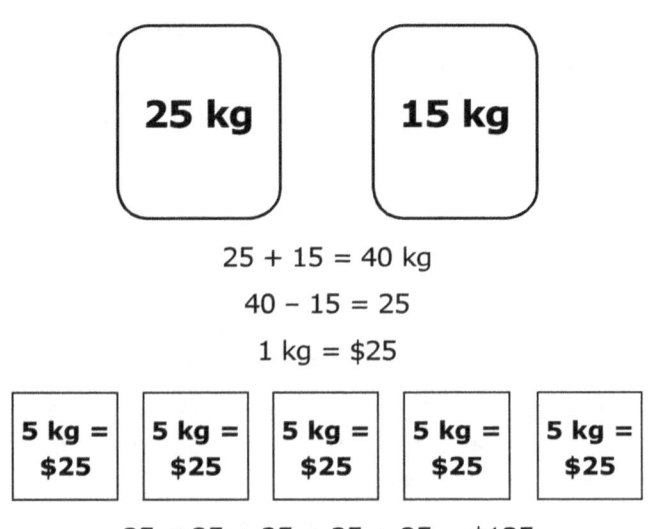

$25 + 15 = 40$ kg

$40 - 15 = 25$

1 kg = \$25

$25 + 25 + 25 + 25 + 25 = \$125$

Appropriate student explanations will indicate a

student's thought process in solving the problem. For example: Harper has a total mass of 40 kilograms of luggage. I know this because I added her bags of luggage together: 15 kilograms + 25 kilograms = 40 kilograms. Next, I subtracted 40 − 15 because the first 15 kilograms of her luggage are free. 40 − 15 = 25. If 1 kilogram will cost $5, then I can multiply $5 and the mass of the rest of her luggage: 5 × 25 = $125.

10. **C.** The key words *on each end of the bar* indicate that the first thing you need to do is add the mass on one side and double it or multiply it by 2.

$$10 + 5 + 2\ ½ = 17\ ½$$
$$17\ ½ + 17\ ½ = 35\ kilograms$$

In order to determine how much more mass he needs to add so that he has a total mass of 75 kilograms, you need to subtract: 75 − 35 = 40 kilograms.

11. **B.** The clue words *each glass* indicate that we are dividing or using repeated subtraction. Many students might be tempted to divide the 6 total liters of hot chocolate by the 4 glasses of hot chocolate: 6 ÷ 4, but will realize that it's difficult to create equal groups in this way.

If students look at each answer, they should realize that answer choice *A* is impossible because it involves multiplication.

They should also realize that answer choice *C* is impossible because 6 ÷ 4 does not equal 4.

In choosing between choice *B* and *D*, students can work with repeated addition to determine which answer is correct.

$$1\ ¼ + 1\ ¼ + 1\ ¼ + 1\ ¼ = 5\ liters$$
$$1\ ½ + 1\ ½ + 1\ ½ + 1\ ½ = 6\ liters$$

12. **C; B.** This can be worth 2 points: 1 point for the correct number of beakers and 1 point for the correct number of milliliters.

The clue words each beaker indicate that we are dividing or using repeated subtraction. Many students might be tempted to divide the total number of milliliters of water by the number of milliliters that can fit in each beaker: 325 ÷ 50: but will realize that it's difficult to create equal groups in this way.

In using repeated subtraction students will see that: 325 − **50** = 275 − **50** = 225 − **50** = 175 − **50** = 125 − **50** = 75 − **50** = 25 − **50** = −25.

This eliminates answer choices *A* and *D*. Students will likely be torn between choosing 6 beakers or 7 beakers. Each bolded number 50 above represents 1 beaker. The answer is 7 beakers because you need to put 25 milliliters into the 7th beaker, even though the 7th beaker will not be filled up all entirely.

In order to determine how many more milliliters of water can fit in the last beaker, students need to see that only 25 milliliters is filled in the 7th beaker. Therefore, students need to subtract the total capacity of the container and the amount that is already filled: 50 milliliters − 25 milliliters = 25 milliliters.

3.MD.B.3. Draw Scaled Picture & Bar Graphs & Solve Problems

1. **B, D.** This question can be worth 2 points: 1 point for each correct answer.

9 students like Reading. There are 5 tallies plus 4 more. Science is the least popular subject because it has the least number of votes, 3.

2. **A, D.** The key indicates that each pawprint is equal to 2 animals.

In order to determine the total number of Blue Jays and Chipmunks, you count by twos for each pawprint: 12 altogether.

There is only half of a pawprint next to the Deer. Half of a pawprint is equal to 1. Therefore, there is one Deer altogether.

3. **D, D.** This question can be worth 2 points: 1 point for each correct answer.

The key indicates that each cookie is equal to 4 desserts.

In order to determine how many more cupcakes than fudge, you need to first find the total number of cupcakes and the total number of fudge. If each cookie is worth 4 desserts, then they sold 20 cupcakes and 12 pieces of fudge.

$$20 − 12 = 8\ more\ cupcakes.$$

There are 6 and a half cookies next to the chocolate chip cookies. If each cookie represents 4 desserts, then half of a cookie represents 2 desserts. Therefore, they sold 26 chocolate chip cookies.

4. **B, D.** This question can be worth 2 points: 1 point for each correct answer.

In order to determine how many coats and mittens were collected, you need to add the total number of coats to the total number of mittens.

The bar graph indicates that 20 coats were collected and 15 pairs of mittens were collected.

$$20 + 15 = 35\ coats\ and\ mittens$$

In order to determine how many boots were collected, you need to recognize that the scale is counting by 5s. The bar for the number of boots is approximately halfway between 5 and 10. Students can estimate that 7 pairs of boots were collected.

5. **D, A.** This question can be worth 2 points: 1 point for each correct answer.

The highest bar is on Thursday. Therefore, Cam read the most number of pages on Thursday.

In order to determine how many more pages Cam read on Monday than Tuesday, you must first determine how many pages he read on Monday and Tuesday. In order to do so, you need to recognize that the scale is counting by 5s. On Monday, the bar is slightly above 25, indicating 26. On Tuesday, the bar is slightly past halfway, indicating 18. Next, you subtract 26-18 = 8 pages more.

6. **B, C.** This question can be worth 2 points: 1 point for each correct answer.

The shortest bar is next to pig, so the least popular farm animal is the pig.

In order to determine how many more students voted for chickens than goats, you must first determine how many students voted for goats and chickens. In order to do so, you need to recognize that the scale is counting by 2s. The bar for goats is between 4 and 6, which indicates 5. The bar for chickens is between the 10 and the 12, which indicates 11. Next, you subtract 11 − 5 = 6 more votes.

7. **Correctly completed pictograph, A, C.** This question can be worth 3 points: 1 point for correctly completing the pictograph, and 1 point for each correct answer.

In order to correctly complete the pictograph, students must recognize that each apple equals 2 fruits. Therefore, students should draw:

       3 apples next to oranges

       2 apples next to bananas

       1 apple next to pears

In order to determine how many more students voted for oranges than pears, you need to subtract the number of students who voted for pears, 2, from the number of students who voted for oranges, 6 − 2 = 4 more students.

In order to determine how many students voted for bananas and pears, you need to add the number of students who voted for bananas, 4, to the number of students who voted for pears, 2:

       4 + 2 = 6 students

8. **Accurately drawn bar graph; erasers and smelly pencils; 102 items.** This question can be worth 2 points: 1 point for a correctly drawn bar graph and 1 point for the correct answer.

A correctly drawn bar graph will show the labels of each school supply on the X axis: erasers, pencil sharpeners, smelly pencils, and pens.

The Y axis should start at 0 and count by 5s by each square all the way up to the top, ending with 40.

The bar for erasers should be drawn halfway between 30 and 40, to indicate 35.

The bar for pencil sharpeners should be drawn directly to the 15.

The bar for the smelly pencils should be drawn directly to the top to indicate 40.

The bar for the pens should be between the 10 and the 15, not exactly halfway, to represent 12.

In order to determine how many items were sold altogether, you add the total number sold for each item: 35 (erasers) + 15 (pencil sharpeners) + 40 (smelly pencils) + 12 (pens) = 102 items altogether

9. **2nd and 4th Choices; A; 3rd and 4th Choices.** This question can be worth 5 points: 1 point for each correct answer.

To determine what teachers have between 300 and 400 books in their classroom libraries, you need to locate the bars that are greater than 300, but less than 400. Mrs. Mullins and Mr. O'Toole have between 300 and 400 books in their classroom libraries. Students should select the 2nd and 4th answer choices.

In order to determine who Carolyn's teacher is, you first need to subtract 100 from 350. Sharon's teacher has about 350 books and Carolyn's teacher has about 100 less. 350 − 100 = 250 books. The teacher that has about 250 books is Mr. Sullivan.

In order to determine the teachers who have between 900 and 1,000 books in their classroom libraries, you need to look at the answer choices and add the number of books in each teacher's library.

Mrs. Mullins, Mrs. Brown, Mr. O'Toole: 375 + 300 + 350 = 1, 025 books

Mrs. Mullins, Mr. O'Toole: 375 + 350 = 725 books

Mr. Sullivan, Mrs. Brown, Mr. O'Toole: 250 + 300 + 350 = 900 books

Mr. Sullivan, Mrs. Mullins, Mr. O'Toole: 250 + 375 + 350 =975

Students should therefore select the 3rd (Mr. Sullivan, Mrs. Brown, Mr. O'Toole) and 4th answer choices (Mr. Sullivan, Mrs. Mullins, Mr. O'Toole).

10. **Correctly drawn bar graph, C, C, 344; Appropriate explanation.** This question can be worth 5 points: 1 point for a correctly drawn bar graph, 1 point for each correct answer, and 1 point for an appropriate explanation.

A correctly drawn bar graph will show the labels of each sport on the X axis: soccer, baseball, football, tennis.

The Y axis should start at 50 and count by 10s by each square all the way up to the top, ending with 130.

The bar for soccer should be drawn just slightly below the 80 to represent 79 students.

The bar for baseball should be drawn between the 90 and 100 to represent 95 students.

The bar for football should be drawn directly to 110.

The bar for tennis should be drawn directly to the 60.

In order to determine how many more students voted for football than tennis, you need to subtract the number of students who voted for tennis, 60, from the number of students who voted for football, 110. 110 − 60 = 50 more students.

In order to determine the order the students voted from least to most favorite, you need to put the sports in order from smallest number of votes to most number of votes: Tennis (60), Soccer (79), Baseball (95), and Football (110).

In order to determine how many students voted altogether, you add the total number of votes for each sport:

$$60 + 79 + 95 + 110 = 344 \text{ students.}$$

An appropriate student explanation may state: I know that 344 students voted altogether. I know this because I added the number of students who voted for tennis (60), plus the number of students who voted for soccer (79), plus the number of students who voted for baseball (95), plus the number of students who voted for football (110) which equals 344 students.

11. **Accurately drawn bar graph, D.** This question can be worth 2 points: 1 point for an accurately drawn bar graph and 1 point for the correct answer

Before you can create the bar graph, you first need to determine how many sports cards each friend has.

Kim has 140 sports cards.

If James has 20 less sports cards than Kim, then he has 120 cards.

If Mark has 30 more cards than James, then he has 150 sports cards.

If Dawn has twice as many sports cards as James, then she has 240 cards.

A correctly drawn bar graph will show the labels of each friend on the X axis: Kim, James, Mark, and Dawn.

The Y axis should start at 100 and count by 20s by each square all the way up to the top, ending with 260.

The bar for Kim should be drawn directly to the 140.

The bar for James should be drawn directly to the 120.

The bar for Mark should be drawn halfway between 140 and 160 to represent 150.

The bar for Dawn should be drawn directly to 240.

In order to determine the number of sports cards the friends have from greatest to least, you need to put the friends in order from largest amount of sports cards to smallest amount of sports cards: Dawn (240), Mark (150), Kim (140), and James (120).

12. **Accurately drawn pictograph; D; Correct order of insects; 1st, 2nd, and 5th Choices.** This question can be worth 5 points: 1 point for an accurately drawn pictograph, 1 point for the correct order of insects, and 3 points for each correct answer

Before you can create the pictograph, you need to determine how many of each type of insects the class caught.

They caught 25 pill bugs.

If they caught twice as many spiders as pill bugs, they caught 50 spiders.

If they caught 25 more ants than spiders, they caught 75 ants.

If they caught 15 less ladybugs than pill bugs, they caught 10 ladybugs.

To accurately draw the pictograph, students must use the correct scale: each ladybug = 10 insects.

Pill bugs: should have 2 ½ ladybugs

Spiders: should have 5 ladybugs

Ants: should have 7 ½ ladybugs

Ladybugs: should have 1 ladybug

The class collected 125 spiders and ants (75 ants and 50 spiders).

The insects they caught in order from least to greatest is: ants (75), spiders (50), pill bugs (25), and ladybugs (10).

In order to determine how many insects the class caught altogether, you need to add the total amount caught for each insect together: 75 + 50 + 25 + 10 = 160 insects.

Students should select the 1st, 2nd, and 5th answer choices because they each represent 160 insects.

3.MD.B.4 Measure Lengths & Create Line Plots

1. **C.** The envelope extends from the end of the ruler to the 3-inch mark.

2. **B.** The videogame controller extends from the end of the ruler to the 3-centimeter mark.

Students may choose 1-centimeter as their answer if they are looking at the inches rather than the centimeters.

3. **D.** The slice of pizza extends from the end of the ruler to between the 2 and 3-inch mark. It measures 2 ½ inches to the nearest ½ inch.

4. **C.** 4 centimeters is the only logical answer for the approximate measurement of a paperclip. 4 miles and 4 feet are too large and 4 millimeters is too small.

5. **1st, 2nd, 4th, and 6th Choices.** This question can be worth 4 points: 1 point for each correct answer.

This question doesn't ask what would be the BEST measurement. It only asks what COULD be used to measure the length of a football field. Feet, inches, yards, meters could all be used to measure the length of a football field.

Miles and kilometers cannot be used because they are longer than the length of a football field.

Students should have chosen the 1st, 2nd, 4th, and 6th answer choices.

6. **D.** The scissors extend from the end of the ruler to between 5 inches and the end of the ruler. To the nearest ¼ inch, the scissors measure 5 ¾ inches.

7. **C, C.** This question can be worth 2 points: 1 point for each correct answer.

2 bunnies jumped 1 foot because there are 2 plots above the 1 foot mark.

The bunnies jumped 2 ¼ feet the most frequently, because there are the most jumps, 3, above that distance.

8. **B, D.** This question can be worth 2 points: 1 point for each correct answer.

In order to determine how much longer the paintbrush is than the pencil, you must first determine how long each object is.

The paintbrush measures 5 inches and the pencil measures 2 ½ inches. You then subtract 2 ½ from 5, so the paintbrush is 2 ½ inches longer than the pencil.

In order to determine how long the paintbrush and the pencil are altogether, you need to add their individual lengths together.

5 (paintbrush) + 2 ½ (pencil) = 7 ½ inches altogether.

9. **Accurately drawn line plot.** In order to accurately draw a line plot, students need to accurately plot each measurement on the ruler.

There should be 2 marks above 6 km.

There should be 1 mark above 3 ½ km.

There should be 1 mark above 2 ½ km.

There should be 1 mark above 4 km.

10. **C, A.** This question can be worth 2 points: 1 point for each correct answer.

In order to determine how many friendship bracelets are less than 11 inches long, you need to count all of the marks less than 11 inches. There are 6 marks less than 11 inches.

In order to determine how many more friendship bracelets were 11 ¼ inches long than 10 ½ inches long, you need to first determine how many bracelets were made at each length.

4 bracelets were 11 ¼ inches long

3 bracelets were 10 ½ inches long

Then you subtract 4 – 3 = 1 more friendship bracelet.

11. **Correctly drawn line plot; Airplanes 1, 5, 6; C.** This question can be worth 5 points: 1 point for a correctly drawn line plot, and 1 point for each correct answer

To correctly draw the line plot, students must place the appropriate number of marks above each measurement.

There should be 3 marks above 10 ¼ inches.

There should be 2 marks above 7 inches.

There should be 1 mark above 13 inches.

There should be 1 mark above 12 ¾ inches.

To determine which airplanes traveled between 8 and 11 inches, you need to look at the measurements of the airplanes in the table.

Airplanes 1, 5, 6 each traveled 10 ¼ inches.

To determine how many fewer airplanes traveled a distance of 8 ½ inches than 10 ¼ inches, you need to first determine how many airplanes traveled each distance.

0 planes traveled 8 ½ inches and 3 airplanes traveled 10 ¼ inches. Therefore, 3 fewer airplanes traveled a distance of 8 ½ inches.

12. **19; less than; B; Appropriate fish lengths.** This question can be worth 5 points: 1 point for each correct answer, and 2 points for each appropriate explanation

In order to determine how many fish Andrew caught, you need to count the number of marks on the line plot: 19 fish altogether.

In order to determine if Andrew caught more fish less than 7 inches or greater than 7 inches, you need to caught the amount of fish he caught at each length.

Andrew caught 14 fish less than 7 inches and 5 fish greater than 7 inches. Therefore, Andrew caught more fish less than 7 inches.

An appropriate student explanation may state: I know that Andrew caught more fish less than 7 inches. I know this because there are more marks below 7 inches than above 7 inches. Andrew caught 14 fish less than 7 inches and only 5 fish greater than 7 inches.

In order to determine how many more fish measured 5 ¾ than 6 ¾ inches, you need to determine how many fish were caught at each length.

Andrew caught 4 fish at 5 ¾ inches and 2 fish at 6 ¾ inches. Then you subtract 4 – 2 = 2 more fish.

The measurements that only had 1 fish are: 4, 4 ¼, 5, 5 ¼, 5 ½, 7 ¾, 8, and 10 inches.

Each of these measurements only has 1 mark above them.

3.MD.C.5. Recognize Area

1. **D.** Area is the measurement of the amount of space a shape takes up.

The rectangle is composed of 8 square units.

2. **A.** The rectangle is composed of 12 square units.

3. **C.** The shape is composed of 6 square units.

4. **D.** The graph paper would have the most square units because it contains 36 square units. The chocolate bar has 8 square units, the tile is 1 square unit, and the window pane is 4 square units.

5. **B.** A beach towel would likely have the greatest area because it is larger and takes up more space than a cellphone cover, an envelope, and a stamp.

6. **Rectangle A, D.** Rectangle A has a greater area than Rectangle B. The area of Rectangle A is 14 square units, and the area of Rectangle B is 12 square units.

We know that Rectangle A has a greater area because it takes up more space.

7. **B.** The area of the figure is 12 square units because it is composed of 12 square units.

8. **3rd, 4th, and 6th Choices.** In order to determine which statements are true, you need to first find the area of each shape.

Rectangle A has an area of 21 square units.

Rectangle B has an area of 24 square units.

Therefore, the 3rd, 4th, and 6th statements are true:

The area of Rectangle B is 24 square units; the area of Rectangle B is greater than the area of Rectangle A, and Rectangle B takes up more space than Rectangle A.

9. **Brett is correct; Appropriate explanation.** This answer can be worth 2 points: 1 point for the correct answer and 1 point for an appropriate explanation.

Brett is correct. You cannot have a square that has an area of 18. This is impossible because 18 is not a square number.

An appropriate student explanation may state: I agree with Brett. I agree with Brett because a square cannot have an area of 18. A square needs to have all equal sides.

A square with side lengths of 4 has an area of 16 and a square with side lengths of 5 has an area of 25. There isn't a square you can make with an area of 18.

10. **Square; Appropriate explanation.** This question can be worth 2 points: 1 point for the correct answer and 1 point for an appropriate explanation.

Before you can determine which shape has a greater area, you first need to determine the area of each shape.

A rectangle with a length of 7 square units and a width of 4 square units has an area of 28 square units.

A square with a length of 6 square units has an area of 36 square units. A square has all equal sides so 6 x 6 = 36.

An appropriate student explanation may state: The square has a bigger area. I know this because the area of the square is 36 square units and the area of the rectangle is 28 square units.

11. **C, 64 square units, 40 square units.** This question can be worth 3 points: 1 point for each correct answer.

Before you can determine how much greater than area of the rectangle is than the square, you first need to determine the area of each shape.

A square with the length of 8 square units has an area of 64 square units. A square has all equal sides so 8 x 8 = 64.

A rectangle with a length of 5 and a width of 8 has an area of 40 square units.

In order to determine how much greater the area of the square than the rectangle is, is to subtract the area of the rectangle, 40, from the area of the square, 64. 64 – 40 = 24 square units.

12. **2nd, 3rd, and 4th Choices; Appropriate explanation.** This question can be worth 4 points:

1 point for each correct answer and 1 point for an appropriate explanation.

Students should select the 2nd, 3rd, and 5th answer choices.

Each of these choices has an area of 42 square units.

The 1st answer choice has an area of 144 square units.

The 4th answer choice has an area of 108 square units.

Answers will vary according to which measurements students think Sam should choose. All answers can be acceptable as long as students can explain their thinking.

An appropriate student explanation may state: I think Sam should choose a length of 7 square units and a width of 6 square units. I think Sam should choose these measurements because they create a rectangle that is easy for gardening. It isn't too wide, nor too long.

3.MD.C.6. Measure Area

1. **C.** The shaded figure is composed of 12 square meters.

Area is the measurement of the amount of space a shape takes up.

2. **A.** The shaded figure is composed of 18 square centimeters.

3. **D.** The shaded figure is composed of 26 square inches.

4. **C.** The figure is composed of 52 square centimeters.

5. **A.** The figure is composed of 48 square meters.

6. **1st, 2nd, and 3rd Choices.** This question can be worth 3 points: 1 point for each correct answer.

Students should select the 1st, 2nd, and 3rd answer choices. Each of these shapes has an area of 12 square inches. The 4th shape has an area of 10 square inches and the 5th shape has an area of 9 square inches.

7. **D.** To calculate the area of this figure, you must first count the total number of whole square inches. There are 10 whole square inches.

Then you need to put together the partial shaded portions to make additional whole square inches. This shape has five ½ square inches, which totals 2 ½ square inches altogether.

When you add 10 + 2 ½ you get the total area of the shape, 12 ½ square inches.

8. **See detailed explanation.** This question can be worth 3 points: 1 point for accurately drawing a shape and 1 point for each correct answer.

Students can draw either a 7 x 2 rectangle or a 2 x 7 rectangle. There isn't enough space to draw anything larger.

9. **A.** To calculate the area of this figure, you must first count the total number of whole square inches. There are 13 whole centimeters.

Then you need to put together the partial shaded portions to make additional whole square centimeters.

There are 10 partial shaded portions left. These can be put together to create 5 additional whole square centimeters.

When you add 13 + 5 = 18 square centimeters.

If students aren't able to match the exact portions, they should still see that the area is closest to 18.

10. **1st, 2nd, and 5th Choices; Appropriate drawing.** This question can be worth 4 points: 1 point for each correct answer and 1 point for an accurate drawing.

Students should select the first, second, and fifth answer choices.

The third answer choice has an area of 20 square inches and the fourth answer choice has an area of 25 square inches.

Students can really only draw a 9 x 2 rectangle. There isn't enough space to draw an 18 x 1 or a 1 x 18 rectangle, and the other choices were listed in the previous question. However, you can accept responses if students choose to draw in additional square units in order to accurately draw a longer rectangle.

11. **B; Appropriate drawing.** This question can be worth 2 points: 1 point for a correct answer and 1 point for an accurate drawing.

To calculate the area of this figure, you must first count the total number of whole square centimeters. There are 26 whole centimeters.

Then you need to put together the partial shaded portions to make additional whole square centimeters.

There are 10 partial portions left. These can put be together to make about 5 more whole square centimeters.

When you add 26 + 5 = 31 square centimeters.

If students aren't able to match the exact portions, they should still see that the area is closest to 31.

Student drawings will vary. Accept student responses as long as the total area of the shape is 31.

12. **C; D; 370 square feet.** In order to determine the order of the snow walls from least to greatest, you first need to find the area of each snow wall.

Cathy: 12 x 10 = 120 square feet

Jay: 120 − 20 = 100 square feet

Destiny: 120 + 30 = 150 square feet

Jay's snow wall is the smallest, followed by Cathy's and Destiny's

In order to determine how much larger Destiny's snow wall is than Jay's, you need to subtract his total area, 100 square feet, from her total area, 150 square feet:

150 − 100 = 50 square feet

In order to find the total area of all 3 snow walls, you add the individual areas together:

150 + 120 + 100 = 370 square feet

3.MD.C.7. Relate Area to Multiplication and Addition

1. **B.** The number sentence 5 + 5 + 5 represents the 3 rows with 5 squares in each row for a total area of 15 square units.

2. **C.** You need to multiply length x width in order to find the total area of the shape.

The length is 4 square units and the width is 3 square units.

Therefore, 4 x 3 = 12 square units.

3. **1st, 3rd, and 5th Choices.** This question can be worth 3 points: 1 point for each correct answer.

Students should select the 1st, 3rd, and 5th answer choices. Each of these answer choices represents an area of 18 square units.

The rectangle has 3 rows with 6 squares in each row for a total of 18 square units.

4. **A.** The area of the rectangle is 24 square units. You multiply the length, 4, times the width, 6.

$$4 \times 6 = 24.$$

5. **2nd, 3rd, and 4th Choices.** This question can be worth 3 points: 1 point for each correct answer.

Students should select the 2nd, 3rd, and 4th answer choices. Each of these answer choices represents an area of 30 square units.

The 1st answer choice has an area of 27 square units and the 5th answer choice has an area of 25 square units.

6. **C.** Students need to determine the width of the basketball court if the length is 8 yards and the total area is 48 square yards.

Students can determine the missing side length by multiplying 8 x N = 48 or 48 ÷ 8 = N.

$$N = 6.$$

7. **A.** Students need to determine the length of the garden if the width is 6 yards and the total area is 54 square yards.

Students can determine the missing side length by multiplying 6 x N = 54 or 54 ÷ 6 = N.

$$N = 9.$$

8. **See detailed explanation; 48 square units.** This question can be worth 4 points: 1 point for each correct answer

This question measures a student's ability to apply their understanding about area to the distributive property of multiplication. The distributive property of multiplication states that the product of multiplying two factors will equal the same thing as breaking up one factor into two addends, multiplying each addend by the other factor, and then adding together both products.

The dimensions of the large rectangle are 4 x 12. When you break down the larger rectangle into two smaller rectangles, you get one rectangle with the dimensions of 4 x 10 and one rectangle with the dimensions of 4 x 2. This can be represented in the following expressions: 40 + 8, 4 x 12, and (4 x 10) + (4 x 2). Therefore, students should select the **3rd, 4th, and 5th answer choices**.

Each of these expressions shows that the total area of the rectangle is 48 square units.

9. **2nd, 3rd, and 4th Choices; 45 square units.** This question can be worth 4 points: 1 point for each correct answer.

This question also measures a student's ability to apply the distributive property to area.

The dimensions of the larger rectangle are 3 x 15.

The line that divides the rectangle into two smaller rectangles, indicates that the first rectangle represents the larger addend that you get when splitting up the number 15.

As students notice the answer choices, they will observe that the 15 is split up into 10 + 5.

This means that the dimensions of the smaller rectangles are: 3 x 10 and 3 x 5. This can be represented in the following expressions: (10 x 3) + (5 x 3), 15 x 3, and 30 + 15. Therefore, students should select the 2nd, 3rd, and 4th answer choices. Each of these expressions shows that the total area of the rectangle is 45 square units.

10. **See detailed explanation; A; D.** This question can be worth 3 points: 1 point for correctly decomposing the shape, and 1 point for each correct answer.

Students can draw a line that decomposing the larger shape into 2 smaller rectangles and 1 square OR 1 smaller rectangle and 2 squares. No matter how students decompose the shape, the value of X is 5 meters.

We know that the value of X is 5 meters because the line that is parallel to the X has a value of 15. When we look at the sides that are then parallel to the 15 meters, we see that 2 of the lines have a value of 5 meters. These 3 sides must be of equivalent to the value of the parallel line, measuring 15 meters. This means the value of X needs to be 5 because 5 + 5 + 5 = 15 meters.

To find the total area of the figure, students need to first find the areas of the 3 smaller figures of the decomposed shape.

If students decompose the larger shape into 2 smaller rectangles and 1 square, the area is found by adding: (5 x 10) + (5 x 10) + (5 x 5) = 125 square meters

If students decompose the larger shape into 1 smaller rectangle and 2 squares, the area is found by adding: (5 x 5) + (5 x 5) + (15 x 5) =125 square meters

11. **See detailed explanation; C; Appropriate explanation; 124 square units.** This question can be worth 4 points: 1 point for correctly decomposing the shape, 1 point for each correct answer, and 1 point for an appropriate explanation

Students can draw lines that decompose this shape into 3 smaller rectangles OR 2 smaller rectangles and 1 square. No matter how students decompose the shape, the value of X is 6 meters.

We know that the value of X is 6 meters because the line that is parallel to the X has a value of 6. We know that opposite sides of a rectangle/square are equal. Therefore, the value of X is 6.

An appropriate student explanation for determining the value of X may state: I know that the value of X is 6 meters. I know this because the line that is parallel and opposite to the X is worth 6 meters, and I know that opposite sides of a rectangle/square have equal lengths.

To find the total area of the figure, students need to first find the areas of the 3 smaller figures of the decomposed shape.

If students decompose the larger shape into 3 smaller rectangles, the area is found by adding: (10 x 2) + (6 x 14) + (2 x 10) = 124 square meters

If students decompose the larger shape into 2 smaller rectangles and 1 square, the area is found by adding: (6 x 2) + (10 x 10) + (6 x 2) = 124 square meters

12. **A; 48 square units; Design A; Appropriate explanation.** This question can be worth 4 points: 1 point for each correct answer and 1 point for an appropriate explanation

In order to determine what expression can be used to find the total area of Design A, students need to compare the answer choices to how you can decompose the shape.

The shape can be decomposed into 2 smaller rectangles with dimensions of: 12 x 3 and 4 x 3 OR 2 smaller rectangles with dimensions of: 6 x 4 and 8 x 3.

No matter how the shape is decomposed, the total area is 48 square units.

Even though letter A does equal 48, it cannot be used to find the total area of Design A. It cannot be used because it doesn't match the dimensions of the rectilinear figure.

In order to determine which design has a greater area, students will also need to find the total area of Design B. The dimensions of Design B are: 4 x 10 ½ for a total area of: 42 square units. If students are unable to multiply fractions/decimals, they can simply count the number of square units in Design B.

Since the area of Design A is 48 square units and the area of Design B is 42 square units, Design A has a greater area.

An appropriate student explanation may state: Design A has a greater area. I know this because the area of Design A is 48 square meters and the area of Design B is 42 square meters.

3.MD.D.8. Solve Problems Involving Perimeter

1. **B.** Perimeter is the measurement of the distance around an object. To determine the perimeter, you add all the side lengths together. The sum is the perimeter of the shape. 2 + 3 + 2 + 3 = 10 units

2. **A.** 3 + 3 + 1 + 1 + 1 + 1 + 1 + 1 = 12 units

3. **C.** 1 + 3 + 3 + 2 + 2 + 1 = 12 units

4. **B.** 5 + 6 + 7 = 18 units

5. **C; 26 units.** This question can be worth 2 points: 1 point for each correct answer.

The correct expression that could be used to find the perimeter of the trapezoid is:

8 + 4 + 8 + 6 for a total perimeter of 26 units.

6. **C.** The missing side length is 6 units. We can figure this out by first adding together the known side lengths: 6 + 6 + 3 = 15. We can then subtract the sum from the total perimeter of the shape: 18. 18 − 15 = 3 units.

Students can also determine the missing side length with what they know about the attributes of rectangles. Students know that opposite sides of a rectangle have the same length.

7. **B.** If the computer lab is in the shape of a hexagon,

that means that there are 6 sides. Each side is 30 feet long. In order to determine the total perimeter, you need to add: 30 + 30 + 30 + 30 + 30 + 30 = 180 OR you can multiply 30 x 6 = 180 feet.

8. **D.** To determine the length of each side of a rhombus, students must first know that all 4 sides of a rhombus are equal. If the perimeter of the rhombus is 32, you simply need to divide 4 into 32:

$$32 \div 4 = 8 \text{ units per side}$$

9. **B; 2nd, 4th, and 5th Choices.** This question can be worth 5 points: 1 point for each correct answer.

To determine the value of the missing side, students need to recognize that the missing side has the same value has its opposite/parallel side. Therefore, the missing side has a length of 4 units.

The expressions that can be used to find the total perimeter of the shape are the: 1st, 2nd, 4th, and 5th.

The expression is the first answer choice is the expression for adding 1 side length at a time.

4 + 2 + 2 + 8 + 2 + 2 + 4 + 2 + 2 + 8 + 2 + 2 = 40 units.

The 2nd, 4th, and 5th answer choices are variations of the first expression. These answer choices have grouped the numbers in different ways to make the addition easier, but all expressions have a sum of 40 units.

10. **2nd, 4th, and 6th Choices; D; C.** This question can be worth 5 points: 1 point for each correct answer.

Since the shape of the banner is going to be a square with a total perimeter of 90 and 100, the only possible answer choices are: 23, 24, and 25.

If each side was 23 feet, the total perimeter would be 92 feet.

If each side was 24 feet, the total perimeter would be 96 feet.

If each side was 25 feet, the total perimeter would be 100.

Therefore, students should select the 2nd, 4th, and 6th answer choices.

If the width of the square banner was 15 feet, then the perimeter would be 60 feet because 15 + 15 + 15 + 15 = 60 feet.

If the width of the square banner was 15 feet, then the area would be 225 square feet because 15 x 15 = 225 square feet.

11. **1st, 3rd, and 4th Choices; 8 inches; Appropriate explanation.** This question can be worth 5 points: 1 point for each correct answer and 1 point for an appropriate explanation.

In order to determine which designs Debbie can choose, students must find the perimeter of each design.

The 1st, 3rd, and 4th designs all have perimeters of 48 units.

The 2nd design has an area of 48 units, not a perimeter of 28 units.

The 5th design has a perimeter of 32 units.

If the cake is in the shape of a hexagon, then each side must be 8 inches long. There are 6 sides on a hexagon, so 6 sides x 8 inches on each side = a perimeter of 48 inches.

An appropriate student explanation may state: I know that each side must be 8 inches long. I know this because a hexagon has 6 sides and all sides are the same length. When you add 8 + 8 + 8 + 8 + 8 + 8, you get a perimeter of 48 inches.

12. **7 units; See detailed explanation;216 square units; 110 units; 106 square units.** This question can be worth 5 points: 1 point for each correct answer.

We know that the value of X is 7 units because the line that is parallel to the x has a value of 15 units. When we look at the sides that are then parallel to the 15 meters, we see that 2 of the lines have a value of 4 units. These 3 sides must be equivalent to the value of the parallel line, measuring 15 meters. This means the value of X needs to be 7 because 4 + 4 + 7 = 15 units.

Students can decompose the larger shape in various ways. As long as the students decompose the shape so that it is only composed of smaller squares and rectangles, then students have decomposed correctly.

In order to find the total area of the shape, students need to find the area of each of the smaller figures and add them together. One example is:

$$(15 \times 4) + (11 \times 4) + (20 \times 7) =$$
$$60 + 44 + 140 = 244 \text{ square units}$$

To find the total perimeter of the shape, students need to add the 8 side lengths together:

$$4 + 4 + 4 + 5 + 7 + 20 + 15 + 15 = 74 \text{ units}$$

In order to determine how much greater the area is than the perimeter, you need to subtract:

$$244 - 74 = 170 \text{ units larger}$$

GEOMETRY

3.G.A.1. Recognize & Understand Shape Categories & Attributes

1. **C.** A quadrilateral is a 4-sided polygon. A quadrilateral also has 4 corners (vertices). Letter C is the only

4-sided shape; therefore, it is a quadrilateral.

2. **C.** Letter *C* is not a quadrilateral because it is a pentagon and it has 5 sides.

3. **See detailed explanation.** This question can be worth up to 8 points: 1 point for each shape that is correctly sorted.

Students should place letters *C*, *D*, *F*, and *H* into the category of quadrilaterals. Each of these shapes has 4 sides and 4 corners.

Students should place letters *A*, *B*, *E*, and *G* into the category of non-quadrilaterals.

4. **1st, 3rd, and 5th Choices.** This question can be worth 4 points: 1 point for each correct answer.

Students should select the 1st, 3rd, and 5th answer choices. A quadrilateral must have 4 sides, 4 corners, and must be a closed figure. A quadrilateral MAY have all equal sides and all square corners, but these are not NECESSARY attributes of a quadrilateral.

5. **D.** This question measures a student's ability to apply their understanding of quadrilateral attributes to different shapes. Since all rhombuses have 4 sides and 4 corners, all rhombuses are quadrilaterals.

6. **C.** A trapezoid has 1 pair of opposite parallel sides and 1 pair of equal sides.

7. **B.** A rectangle has 2 lines of symmetry, 4 square corners, and equal opposite sides. While a square has 4 square corners and equal opposite sides, a square has 4 lines of symmetry rather than 2.

8. **D; 2nd, 3rd, 4th, and 5th Choices.** This question can be worth 5 points: 1 point for each correct answer.

The shape is a parallelogram. A parallelogram is a shape that has 4 sides, with opposite sides parallel/congruent. Therefore, students should choose the 2nd, 3rd, 4th, and 5th answer choices as attributes of a parallelogram. While it is possible for a parallelogram to have all equal sides and all square corners, they are not necessary attributes of a parallelogram.

9. **See detailed explanation.** This question can be worth 3 points: 1 point for the correct answer, 1 point for an appropriate drawing, and 1 point for an appropriate explanation.

Joy is correct. An appropriate student explanation may state:

Joy is correct. I know this because a quadrilateral is a shape with 4 sides and 4 corners. All squares have 4 sides and 4 corners, so all squares are quadrilaterals. Erin is wrong because quadrilaterals can also be rectangles, rhombuses, and trapezoids.

An appropriate student illustration should show an example of a square as a quadrilateral as well as another example of a quadrilateral: rectangle, trapezoid, diamond, kite, rhombus, parallelogram

10. **C.** This question measures a student's ability to apply their understanding of shape attributes to various categories of shapes. All rhombuses, squares, and rectangles are parallelograms. Parallelograms are shapes with 4 sides, with opposite sides parallel/congruent.

11. **A.** This question measures a student's ability to apply their understanding of shape attributes to various categories of shapes. The attributes of rectangles are 4 square corners and opposite sides equal. Therefore, all squares are rectangles. All rectangles cannot be squares because all sides must be equal. All rhombuses cannot be rectangles because rhombuses must have all congruent sides. All rhombuses cannot be squares because rhombuses do NOT have to have square corners.

12. **1st, 5th, and 6th Choices.** This question can be worth 5 points: 1 point for each correct answer and 1 point for a correctly drawn shape.

The image most directly relates to a rectangle: 4 square corners and opposite sides equal. This shape also has the same attributes as a parallelogram and quadrilateral.

Students should draw a shape that has 4 square corners and opposite sides equal.

3.G.A.2. Partition Shapes & Represent Parts as Fractions

1. **C.** Letter C is divided into equal parts. The line segments partition the shape into 2 equal parts.

2. **C.** The star is divided into 2 equal parts. 1 equal part is shaded, creating the fraction $1/2$.

3. **D.** Letter D is divided into 3 equal parts and 1 part is shaded.

Letter *A* is divided into 3 parts and has 1 part shaded. However, the parts are not equal.

Letter *B* is divided into 6 parts and has 2 parts shaded, but the parts are not equal.

Letter *C* is divided into 3 equal parts, but all 3 parts are shaded.

4. **2nd and 3rd Choices.** This question can be worth 3 points: 1 point for each correct answer and 1 point for an appropriate explanation.

Students should choose the 2nd and 3rd answer choices. These are the only 2 shapes that are divided into 4 equal parts.

An appropriate student explanation may state: I know that the star is partitioned into fourths. I know this because it is divided into 4 parts and each part has an equal area.

5. See detailed explanation. This question can be worth 2 points: 1 point for correctly partitioning the shape and 1 point for correctly shading the shape.

Students should partition the circle into 3 equal parts similar to below:

Students then need to shade 2 portions to show the fraction $2/3$.

6. B. The shape is divided into 6 equal parts. Therefore, each part is a fraction representing $1/6$.

7. A; See detailed explanation. This question can be worth 2 points: 1 point for the correct answer and 1 point for correctly shading the shape.

The circle is divided into 8 equal parts. Therefore, each part is a fraction representing $1/8$.

To show the fraction $3/8$, students should shade 3 parts of the total shape.

8. 1st, 3rd, 5th and 6th Choices. This question can be worth 4 points: 1 point for each correct answer.

Students should choose the 1st, 3rd, 5th and 6th answer choices. The shape contains 24 equal parts and 8 parts are shaded: $8/24$. This fraction can also be represented as (or is equivalent to) the fractions $4/12$, $2/6$, and $1/3$.

9. B. If the total area of the figure is 60 square units and you are trying to determine $1/3$ of the total area, you need to divide: 60 ÷ 3 = 20. The area of $1/3$ of the total shape is 20 square units.

10. D. If the total area of the rectangle is 54 square feet and you are trying to determine the area of the shaded portion, you first need to determine how much each shaded portion is worth.

If the total area of the rectangle is 54 square feet and it is portioned into 6 equal parts, then each part is equal to 9 square feet. 54 ÷ 6 = 9.

If 4 of the 6 parts are shaded, you need to multiply 4 x 9 = 36. Therefore, 36 square feet of the total area is shaded.

11. B; C. This question can be worth 2 points: 1 point for each correct answer.

If the total area of the rectangle is 72 square feet and you are trying to determine the area of the shaded portion, you first need to determine how much each shaded portion is worth.

If the total area of the rectangle is 72 square feet and it is partitioned into 6 equal parts, then each part is equal to 12 square feet. 72 ÷ 6 = 12.

If 1 of the 6 parts is shaded, you need to multiply 1 x 12 = 12. Therefore, 12 square feet of the total area is shaded.

In order to determine how many more parts need to be shaded in order to have an area of 48 square feet, you need to divide. If each part is worth 12 square feet, you need to divide: 48 ÷ 12 = 4 parts. If 4 parts need to be shaded to show an area of 48 square feet and 1 part is already shaded, that means 3 more parts need to be shaded.

12. See detailed explanation. This question can be worth 2 points: 1 point for shading in the correct portion and 1 point for an appropriate explanation.

If the total area of the rectangle is 120 square feet and you are trying to shade an area of 75 square feet, you first need to determine how much each shaded portion is worth.

If the total area of the rectangle is 120 square feet and it is partitioned into 8 equal parts, then each part is equal to 15 square feet. 120 ÷ 8 = 15.

If you need to shade an area of 75 square feet, you need to divide: 75 ÷ 15 = 5. Therefore, you need to shade 5 parts of the rectangle.

An appropriate student explanation may state: I know I need to shade 5 parts of the rectangle because each part is worth 15 square feet. I know this because the total area of the shape is 120 square feet and the rectangle is divided into 8 equal parts. 120 ÷ 8 = 15. Then I figured out 15 x ? = 75. I know 15 x 5 = 75, so I know I have to shade in 5 parts.

PRACTICE TEST

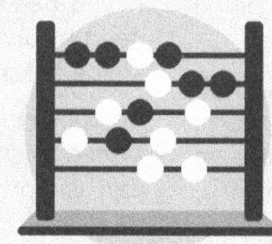

ACT ASPIRE
Mathematics
Practice Test One

1. What unknown number makes this equation true?

   $\square = 346 - 118$

   Ⓐ 464
   Ⓑ 228
   Ⓒ 232
   Ⓓ 454

2. Brady picked 24 apples. He put them in 4 baskets. He put the same number of apples in each basket. How many apples did he put in each basket?
   Ⓐ 6
   Ⓑ 4
   Ⓒ 20
   Ⓓ 24

3. Which expression is equal to 4 x 5, and why?
   Ⓐ 4 ÷ 5, because multiplication and division are inverse operations
   Ⓑ 5 + 4, because the order of numbers does not matter in addition
   Ⓒ 5 x 4, because the order of numbers does not matter in multiplication
   Ⓓ 4 + 5, because the numbers are in the same order

4. Use the information provided to answer Part A, Part B, and Part C for question 4.

   Cory placed point *A* on the number line.

   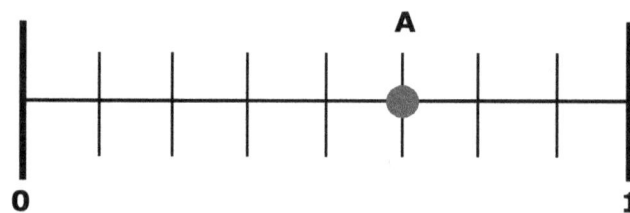

Part A

Give the value of point *A*

Answer: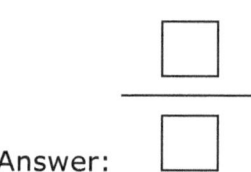

Part B

What does the denominator of your fraction represent on the number line?

_____

_____

Part C
What does the numerator of your fraction represent on the number line?

_____

_____

5. The Third Grade Class visited the local aquarium on a field trip. They took data about the different types of tropical fish they observed. The pictograph below shows how many of each type of fish they saw.

Type of Fish	Number of Fish
Clownfish	🐟 🐟 🐟 🐟 🐟 🐟
Angelfish	🐟 🐟 🐟 🐟
Pufferfish	🐟 🐟 🐟
Brackish Fish	🐟 🐟 🐟 🐟

Each 🐟 = 10 fish

Rob said they saw 35 of his favorite fish. What is Rob's favorite fish? Explain how you know.

_____

_____

_____

6. Look at the time on this clock.

Select the time, to the nearest minute, shown on the clock.
- Ⓐ 3:57
- Ⓑ 11:15
- Ⓒ 3:55
- Ⓓ 2:57

7. The side lengths of a shape are shown.

```
                          11 ft.
                    4 ft.
          7 ft.                                8 ft.
4 ft.
                          18 ft.
```

What is the perimeter of the shape above?

Answer: _____ ft.

8. Carly is taking a group of her friends to an amusement park for her birthday.
    • Carly invites 14 friends.
    • 5 adults are going on the trip.
    • The children and adults will all travel together in cars.
    • Each car can hold 4 people.
    • There must be at least 1 parent in each car.

   What is the fewest number of cars they need?

   Answer: _____

9. Select **ALL** the fractions that are equivalent to 1 whole.
   ☐ $1/3$
   ☐ $6/6$
   ☐ $1/1$
   ☐ $1/3$
   ☐ $3/3$

PRACTICE TEST ONE

10. The town park wants to build a dog park. Two possible designs for the dog park are located on the grid below. Each unit length on the grid equals a length of 1 foot.

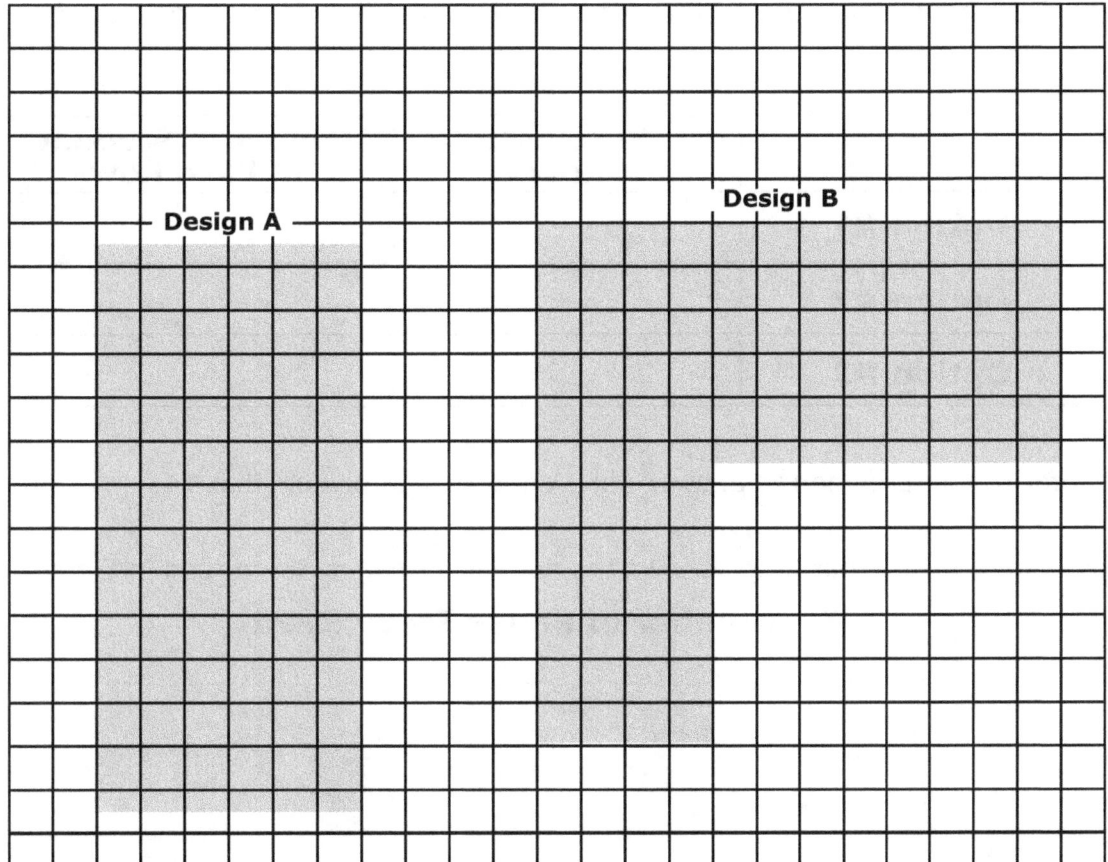

How much more area does Design B have than Design A?
- Ⓐ The areas are equal.
- Ⓑ 4 square feet
- Ⓒ Design A has a greater area than Design B.
- Ⓓ 8.5 square feet

11. What is the value of the unknown number in the equation 9 × 3 = ☐ ?
- Ⓐ 3
- Ⓑ 27
- Ⓒ 11
- Ⓓ 6

12. What number goes in the box to make the equation true?

$$\frac{\square}{1} = 8$$

Answer: _____

13. There are 72 students in the school choir. The music teacher wants to arrange the students in equal rows.

    Complete the table to show three different ways the music teacher could arrange the choir students.

	Number of Rows	Number of Students in Each Row
Option #1		
Option #2		
Option #3		

14. Use the information provided to answer Part A and Part B for question 14.

    Steve loves to read. The bar graph shows the number of pages Steve read in 5 days last week.

    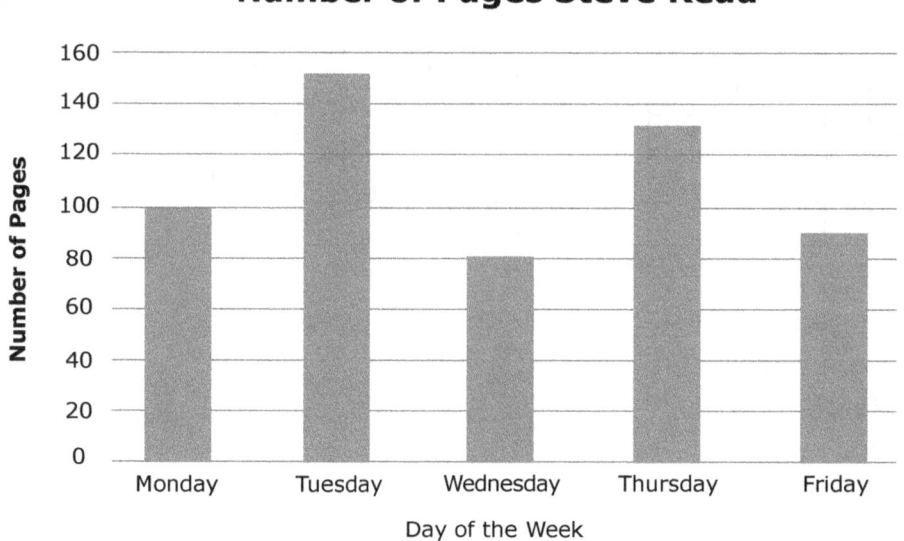

Part A
What is the total number of pages Steve read on Monday and Thursday?
- Ⓐ 30 pages
- Ⓑ 230 pages
- Ⓒ 250 pages
- Ⓓ 50 pages

Part B
How many more pages did Steve read on Tuesday than Friday?
- Ⓐ 60 pages
- Ⓑ 150 pages
- Ⓒ 90 pages
- Ⓓ 240 pages

15. **Part A**

Place each fraction on the number lines below.

Part B

Are these fractions equivalent? Explain how you know.

_____
_____

16. Miranda needs to be at the bus stop by 8:15 in the morning. If Miranda wakes up at 6:45, how much time does Miranda have to get ready?
    - Ⓐ 45 minutes
    - Ⓑ 1 hour
    - Ⓒ 1 hour 30 minutes
    - Ⓓ 1 hour 45 minutes

17. Which of the following numbers round to 200 when rounding to the nearest hundred? Choose **ALL** answers that apply.
    - ☐ 150
    - ☐ 250
    - ☐ 175
    - ☐ 210
    - ☐ 145

18. Becky drew a picture of a trapezoid. She says that all quadrilaterals are trapezoids because they have 4 sides. Draw a picture of a trapezoid and explain whether you agree or disagree with Becky.

_____
_____

19. Oliver and Conner are having a block building contest. The winning design will have the greatest perimeter. Oliver is building a design that is an octagon. Each side is 12 inches long. Conner is building a design that is a pentagon. Each side 15 square inches.

    Who will be the winner of the block building contest?
    - Ⓐ It is a tie, because the perimeters are the same.
    - Ⓑ Conner, because his perimeter is 3 inches more.
    - Ⓒ Oliver, because his perimeter is 21 inches more.
    - Ⓓ Conner, because his design has longer sides.

20. Choose the number that could make each of the statements below true.

    $$N \div 6 = 4$$
    $$3 \times 8 = N$$
    $$N \div 2 = 12$$

    N = _____

21. Match each equation to the correct use of the properties of multiplication.

9 x 7	(2 x 3) x 4
6 x 8	(8 x 4) + (8 x 2)
(4 x 3) x 2	(10 x 6) + (10 x 6)
10 x 12	7 x 9

22. Gabby and Lucas each have water in a beaker.

    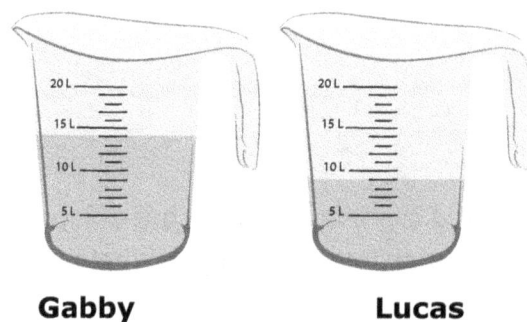

    Gabby　　　　**Lucas**

    About how many more liters of water does Lucas need to have the same amount as Gabby?
    - Ⓐ 15 L
    - Ⓑ 10 L
    - Ⓒ 5 L
    - Ⓓ 0 L

23. Jonah collects change in 4 different jars: 1 jar for pennies, 1 jar for nickels, 1 jar for dimes, and 1 jar for quarters. At the end of the month, Jonah counted all his coins. The table below shows how many of each type of coin Jonah collected.

Type of Coin	Number of Coins
Penny	59
Nickel	25
Dime	18
Quarter	15

Part A
Jonah wants to buy a new basketball for $5.50. Does Jonah have enough money? Explain how you know.

_____

_____

_____

Part B
Jonah uses some of his nickels to buy candy. After buying candy, Jonah has 10 nickels left. How much money did Jonah spend on candy?

Answer: _____

24. Label where the fraction ³/₁ belongs on the number line above. Draw a point to show the fraction.

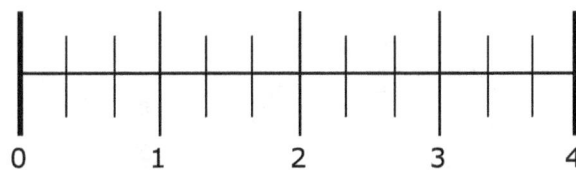

25. A model of a playground is shown below. Draw lines to show you would can decompose the figure to find the total area of the playground.

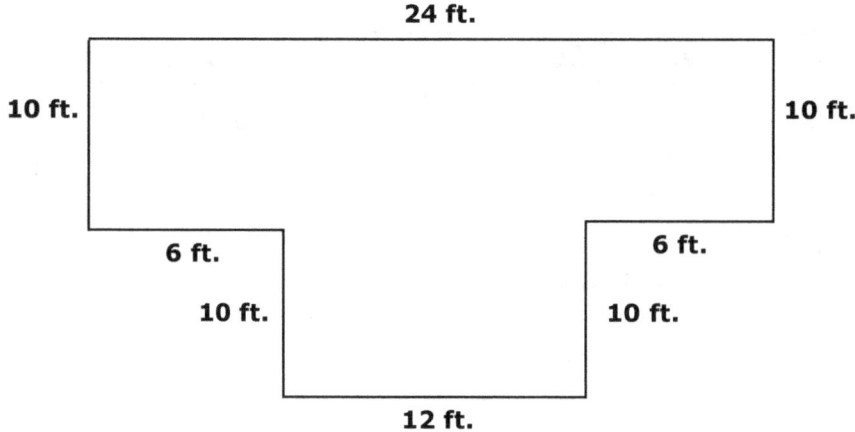

Write the total area of the playground.

Answer: _____ square feet

26. Jade is baking cookies. She prepares them on a cookie tray in 6 rows with 7 cookies in each row. How many cookies did Jade bake altogether?

Answer: _____

27. Jose drew this shape and shaded one part.

He says, "I divided the shape into 4 parts. I shaded 1 part. So 1/4 of the shape is shaded." Is Jose correct? Select the statement that explains why or why not.
- Ⓐ Yes, because the largest part is shaded.
- Ⓑ Yes, because there are 4 parts altogether.
- Ⓒ No, because the 4 parts need to be the same size.
- Ⓒ No, because the smallest part should be shaded.

28. How much time has passed from Clock A to Clock B?

- Ⓐ 3 hours
- Ⓑ 3 hours and 52 minutes
- Ⓒ 3 hours
- Ⓒ 2 hours and 52 minutes

29. Which equation has the same unknown value as 48 ÷ ☐ = 6?
   Ⓐ 6 ÷ 48 = ☐
   Ⓑ 6 × ☐ = 48
   Ⓒ 6 × 48 = ☐
   Ⓓ 6 ÷ ☐ = 48

30. Shannon said the answer to the problem 2 x 3 x 4 = 14. Her work is shown:
   • Step 1: 2 x 3 = 6
   • Step 2: 2 x 4 = 8
   • Step 3: 6 + 8 = 14

   Which is true?
   Ⓐ Shannon is incorrect because she multiplied 2 x 3 and 2 x 4.
   Ⓑ Shannon is correct because 6 + 8 = 14.
   Ⓒ Shannon is incorrect because she should have multiplied 6 x 8.
   Ⓓ Shannon is correct because 2 + 4 = 6 and 6 + 8 = 14.

31. Students measured objects around the classroom. They used this data to make a line plot.

Object	Length (in)
Scissors	6 3/4 in.
Highlighter	5 1/4 in.
Calculator	6 3/4 in.
Stapler	5 in.
White Board Eraser	5 in.

   Create a line plot that shows the measurements of the different objects.

   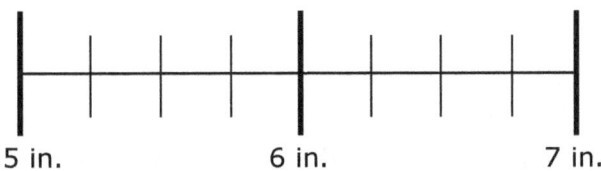

   Measurement of Objects (inches)

32. A pizza has 8 slices. 2 slices are pepperoni, 2 slices are meatball, and the rest are plain cheese. Shade the figure below to show the fraction of the pizza that is plain cheese.

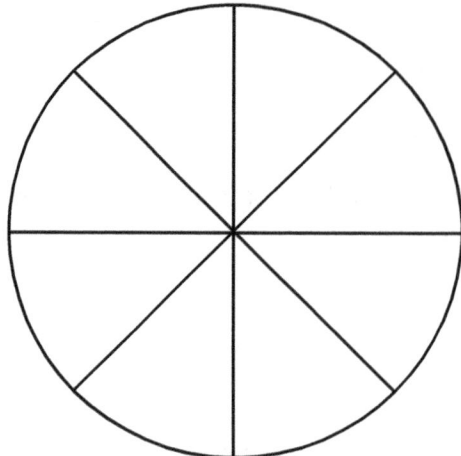

33. Michael scored 20 points in basketball. Dante scored twice as many points as Michael. How any points did they score altogether?
    Ⓐ 40 points
    Ⓑ 60 points
    Ⓒ 22 points
    Ⓓ 20 points

34. The area of the entire rectangle below is 150 square feet.

    Shade the rectangle to show an area of 60 square feet.

35. 10,000 adults, boys, and girls attended a parade. There were 4,389 boys and 4,350 girls. Choose **ALL** the expressions that could be used to find out how many adults were at the parade.

    ☐ 10,000 − 4,389 − 4, 350 = a

    ☐ 4,389 + 4,350 + 10,000 = a

    ☐ 4,389 + 4,350 = 8,739
        10,000 − 8,739 = a

    ☐ 4,389 − 4,350 = 39
        10,000 − 39 = a

    ☐ 10,000 − 4,389 = 5,611
        5,611 − 4,350 = a

36. Monique is buying crayons in boxes of 8 and 24. She wants to buy a total of 56 crayons. How many of each kind of crayon box does she need to buy?

    Answer: _____

37. Mrs. Carter is arranging the desks in her classroom. She has 30 students, and she wants all the rows to be equal. Which layout is NOT possible?
    Ⓐ 5 rows, 6 students in each row
    Ⓑ 6 rows, 5 students in each row
    Ⓒ 3 rows, 10 students in each row
    Ⓓ 10 rows, 30 students in each row

38. Complete the chart below.

x	5x	6x	7x	8x	9x	10x
20	100					

Mathematics Practice Test One Answer Key & Explanations

Mathematics Practice Test One
Answer Explanations

1. **B.** 346 − 118 = 228 Due to the unknown variable being placed at the beginning of the number sentence, students may misinterpret the question as: X − 346 = 118. In this case, they may add instead of subtract.
Difficulty Level: Medium
Standard: 3.NBT.A.2

2. **A.** The clue words *same number* and *each* indicate that repeated subtraction/division is required to answer the question.
24 ÷ 6 = 4 apples in each basket
24 − 6 − 6 − 6 − 6 = 4 apples in each basket
Difficulty Level: Easy
Standard: 3.OA.A.3

3. **C.** This question measures student understanding of the commutative property. 4 x 5 and 5 x 4 mean the same thing because the commutative property states that you can switch the order of the factors and the product will not change.
Difficulty Level: Easy
Standard: 3.OA.B.5

4. **See detailed explanation. Part A:** The number line begins at 0, ends at 1, and is divided into 8 equal parts. Point A is located on the 5th tick mark, indicating the fraction 5/8.

Part B: The denominator of the fraction, 8, indicates that there are 8 total segments in the whole.

Part C: The numerator of the fraction, 5, indicates that we are counting 5 parts, or segments, of the whole.
Difficulty Level: Medium
Standard: 3.NF.A.2

5. **Brackish Fish; Appropriate explanation.** The key states that each fish symbol is worth 10 fish. Therefore, each ½ of a fish symbol is worth 5 fish. There are 3 and ½ fish symbols next to the Brackish Fish, which equals 35 total fish.

An appropriate student explanation may state: I know that Rob's favorite fish is the Brackish Fish. I know this because each fish symbol is worth 10 fish and there are 3 ½ fish symbols next to the Brackish fish. The ½ fish symbol is worth 5 fish. So, 10 + 10 + 10 + 5 = 35 fish.
Difficulty Level: Medium
Standard: 3.MD.B.3

6. **D.** This clock shows 2:57. The hour hand is between the hours 2 and 3. The minute hand is 2 minutes past the 11, which signifies 57 minutes past the hour. Therefore, the time is 2:57.
Difficulty Level: Easy
Standard: 3.MD.A.1

7. **52 feet.** Perimeter is the measurement the distance around an object. To determine the perimeter of this shape, you need to add each of the lengths together: 18 + 8 + 11 + 4 + 7 + 4 = 52 feet
Difficulty Level: Medium
Standard: 3.MD.D.8

8. **5 cars.** If Carly invites 14 friends to her birthday party, there will be 15 children altogether, including Carly. If 4 people can fit in 1 car and at least 1 adult needs to be in each car, then each car can only carry 3 children. Each car can carry 1 adult and 3 children.

2 cars: carries 2 adults and 6 children altogether.
3 cars: carries 3 adults and 9 children altogether.
4 cars: carries 4 adults and 12 children altogether.
5 cars: carries 5 adults and 15 children altogether
Difficulty Level: Hard
Standard: 3.OA.D.8

9. **2nd, 3rd and 5th Choices.** Fractions that are equivalent to 1 whole have the same numerator and the same denominator. $6/6$, $1/1$, and $3/3$ are all equivalent to 1 whole.
Difficulty Level: Medium
Standard: 3.NF.A.3

10. **D.** To determine how much greater the area of Design B is than Design A, you first need to determine the area of each design. Design A has a length of 13 feet (12 full units and 2 half units to total 13 units) and a width of 6 feet: 13 x 6 = 78 square feet.

To determine the area of Design B, you need to decompose the shape into 2 smaller rectangles. One way to do this creates a 4 x 11 rectangle and a 8 x 5.5 rectangle.

4 x 11 = 44 and 8 x 5.5 = 42.5
44 + 42.5 = 86.5 square feet

Lastly, to determine how much greater the area of Design B is than Design A, you need to subtract: 86.5 − 78 = 8.5 square feet
Difficulty Level: Hard
Standard: 3.MD.C.7

11. **B.** 9 x 3 = 27
Difficulty Level: Easy
Standard: 3.OA.A.4

12. **8.** When the numerator of a fraction is larger than the denominator, the fraction is greater than one whole. To represent 8 wholes as a fraction, you

need a numerator of 8 and denominator of 1.
Difficulty Level: Easy
Standard: 3.NF.A.3

13. **Appropriate solutions.** Answers will vary. Possible solutions are:

Number of Rows	Number of Students in Each Row
1	72
2	36
3	24
4	18
6	12
8	9
9	8
12	6
18	4
24	3
36	2
72	1

Difficulty Level: Medium
Standard: 3.OA.A.3

14. Part A: **B;** Part B: **A.**

To determine the total number of pages Steve read on Monday and Thursday, you need to add the number of pages read on Monday, 100, to the number of pages read on Thursday, 130. 100 + 130 = 230 pages. To determine how many more pages Steve read on Tuesday than on Friday, you need to subtract the number of pages read on Friday, 90, from the number of pages read on Tuesday, 150. 150 – 90 = 60 more pages.

Difficulty Level: Medium
Standard: 3.MD.B.3

15. **Correctly drawn number lines; Appropriate explanation. Part A:** Student number lines should resemble the number lines below:

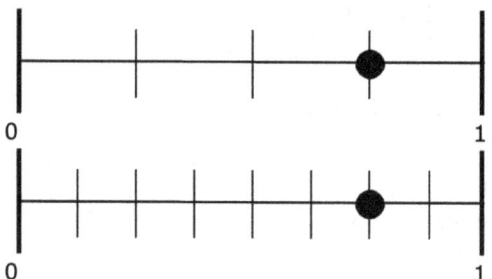

An appropriate student explanation may state: I know that the fractions $^3/_4$ and $^6/_8$ are equivalent. I know this because they represent the same point on the number line.

Difficulty Level: Medium
Standard: 3.NF.A.3

16. **C.** To determine how much time Miranda has to get ready, you need to find the elapsed time between 6:45 and 8:15. An hour and 30 minutes passes from 6:45 to 8:15.

Difficulty Level: Medium
Standard: 3.MD.A.1

17. **1st, 3rd and 4th Choices.** 150 and 175 round up to 200 when rounding to the nearest hundred. The 5 and the 7 in the tens place of each number indicates that you need to round up to the next hundred.

210 rounds down to 200 when rounding to the nearest hundred. The 1 in the tens place indicates that you need to round down to the previous hundred.

Difficulty Level: Easy
Standard: 3.NBT.A.1

18. **Appropriate drawing; Appropriate illustration.** Students should draw a trapezoid that resembles the picture below:

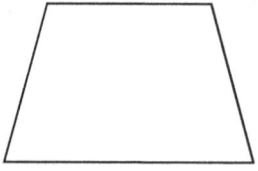

An appropriate student explanation may state: I do not agree with Becky. I do not agree with Becky because not all quadrilaterals have to be trapezoids. For example, squares, rectangles, and parallelograms are also quadrilaterals, but they are not trapezoids.

Difficulty Level: Medium
Standard: 3.G.A.1

19. **C.** In order to determine which student is the winner, you need to find the perimeter of each design.

Oliver's shape has 8 sides and each side is 12 square centimeters long: 12 + 12 + 12 + 12 + 12 + 12 + 12 + 12 = 96 inches.

Conner's shape has 5 sides and each side is 15 square centimeters long: 15 + 15 + 15 + 15 + 15 = 75 inches.

96 – 75 = 21. Oliver's design has a perimeter that is 21 inches greater than Conner's.

Difficulty Level: Hard
Standard: 3.MD.D.8

20. **N = 24.** The only number that makes each number sentence true is 24.

N ÷ 6 = 4

24 ÷ 6 = 4

3 x 8 = N

3 x 8 = 24

N ÷ 2 = 12

24 ÷ 2 = 12

Difficulty Level: Medium
Standard: 3.OA.A.4

21. **Appropriately matched equations.** Students should match 9 x 7 and 7 x 9 because they demonstrate the commutative property: 9 x 7 = 63 and 7 x 9 = 63

Students should match 6 x 8 and (8 x 4) + (8 x 2), because they demonstrate the distributive property: 6 x 8 = 32 + 16 = 48

Students should match (4 x 3) x 2 and (2 x 3) x 4 because they demonstrate the associative property: (4 x 3) x 2 = 12 x 2 = 24 and

(2 x 3) x 4 = 6 x 4 = 24

Students should match 10 x 12 and (10 x 6) + (10 x 6) because they demonstrate the distributive property: 10 x 12 = 60 + 60 = 120

Difficulty Level: Medium
Standard: 3.OA.B.5

22. **C.** To determine how many more liters of water Lucas needs to have the same amount as Gabby, you need to first to determine how much water they each have. Lucas has about 9 liters of water. The shaded part comes just below the 10 L mark. Gabby has about 14 L of water. The shaded part comes just below the 15 L mark. If Lucas has 9 liters of water, he needs 5 more liters to have 14 liters of water.

Difficulty Level: Medium
Standard: 3.MD.A.2

23. **Ye; Appropriate explanation; 75 cents.** Part A: In order to determine if Jonah has enough money to buy a basketball for $5.50, you need to first find out how much money he collected altogether. 59 pennies = 59 cents

25 nickels = .05 x 25 = $1.25

18 dimes = .10 x 18 = $1.80

15 quarters = .25 x 15 = $3.75

Add each of these amounts together: .59 + $1.25 + $1.80 + $3.75 = $7.39.

An appropriate student explanation may state: Jonah has enough money to buy a basketball for $5.50. I know this because he has $7.39 altogether. 59 pennies + $1.25 in nickels + $1.80 in dimes + $3.75 in quarters = $7.39 altogether.

Part B: Jonah has 25 nickels. After buying candy, he has 10 nickels. This means he spent 15 nickels on candy. 15 nickels = .05 x 15 = .75. Jonah spent 75 cents on candy.

Difficulty Level: Hard
Standard: 3.OA.D.8

24. **Correct label on number line.** The number line starts at 0 and ends at 4. The fraction $3/1$ represents 3 wholes. Students should draw a point on the tick mark on the 3.

Difficulty Level: Medium
Standard: 3.NF.A.2

25. **360 square feet.** Students should decompose the larger figure into smaller squares and rectangles. For example, students can decompose the larger figure into 2 smaller rectangles. In this case, 1 rectangle has a length and width of 24 x 10 and the second rectangle has a length and width of 12 x 10. 240 + 120 = 360 square feet.

Difficulty Level: Hard
Standard: 3.MD.C.7

26. **42 cookies.** To determine how many cookies Jade baked altogether, you need to multiply the number of rows of cookies by the number of cookies in each row: 6 x 7 = 42 cookies.

Difficulty Level: Easy
Standard: 3.OA.A.3

27. **C.** The shape is not partitioned correctly because the parts are not equal. Therefore, Jose did not shade $1/4$ of the shape.

Difficulty Level: Easy
Standard: 3.G.A.2

28. **D.** Clock A shows the time 11:57. Clock B shows the time 2:48. 2 hours and 52 minutes passes between Clock A and Clock B.

Difficulty Level: Medium
Standard: 3.MD.A.1

29. **B.** This question measures a student's ability to apply their understanding of the inverse relationship of multiplication and division. 48 ÷ ☐ = 6 is the same thing as 6 x ☐ = 48.

48 ÷ 8 = 6 and 6 x 8 = 48.

Difficulty Level: Easy
Standard: 3.OA.A.4

30. **A.** This question measures a student's ability to apply their understanding of the properties of multiplication. You need to multiply 2 x 3 = 6 and 6 x 4 = 24. Shannon is incorrect because she tried to

use the distributive property to solve the problem instead.

Difficulty Level: Medium
Standard: 3.OA.D.9

31. **Accurately drawn line plot.** To correctly draw the line plot, students must place the appropriate number of marks above each measurement.

There should be 2 marks above 6 ¾ inches.

There should be 1 marks above 5 ¼ inches.

There should be 2 marks above 5 inches.

Difficulty Level: Medium
Standard: 3.MD.B.4

32. **Accurately shaded figure.** If a pizza has 8 slices and 2 of them are pepperoni and 2 of them are meatball, that means the remaining 4 slices are plain cheese. To show this fraction on the figure, students need to shade 4 parts.

Difficulty Level: Medium
Standard: 3.NF.A.1

33. **B.** If Michael scored 20 points, and Dante scored twice as many points as Michael, then Dante scored 40 points. 40 + 20 = 60 points altogether

Difficulty Level: Medium
Standard: 3.NF.A.3

34. **Accurately shaded shape.** If the total area of the rectangle is 150 square feet and you are trying to shade an area of 60 square feet, you first need to determine how much each shaded portion is worth.

If the total area of the rectangle is 150 square feet and it is partitioned into 5 equal parts, then each part is equal to 30 square feet. 150 ÷ 5 = 30.

If you need to shade an area of 60 square feet, you need to divide: 60 ÷ 30 = 2. Therefore, you need to shade 2 parts of the rectangle.

Difficulty Level: Hard
Standard: 3.G.A.2

35. **See detailed explanation.** This problem can be solved by using the **1st, 3rd, and 5th answer choices**. To determine how many adults were at the parade, you can simply subtract the number of boys and the number of girls from the total number of people at the parade: 10,000 − 4,389 − 4,350 = 1,261 adults (1st answer choice) You can also do this by two separate subtraction equations: 10,000 − 4,389 = 5,611 and 5,611 − 4,350 = 1,261 adults (5th answer choice)

You can also add the number of boys and girls that attended the parade altogether: 4,389 + 4,350 = 8,739 and then subtract that from 10,000: 10,000 − 8,738 = 1,261 (3rd answer choice)

Difficulty Level: Medium
Standard: 3.OA.D.8

36. **D. 2 packs of 24; 1 pack of 8 OR 1 pack of 24; 4 packs of 8.** Students can solve this problem in 2 different ways.

2 packs of 24, 1 pack of 8 = 48 + 8 = 56 crayons

OR

1 pack of 24, 4 packs of 8 = 24 + 32 = 56 crayons

Difficulty Level: Medium
Standard: 3.OA.D.8

37. **D.** Letter *D* is not a possible layout because 10 rows and 30 students in each row is 300 students altogether.

Difficulty Level: Medium
Standard: 3.OA.A.3

38. **Accurately filled in table.** Student tables should resemble the table below:

x	5x	6x	7x	8x	9x	10x
20	100	120	140	160	180	200

Difficulty Level: Medium
Standard: 3.NBT.A.3

BONUS
FULL-LENGTH PRACTICE TEST

GO TO THE FOLLOWING URL ADDRESS TO ACCESS YOUR BONUS PRACTICE TEST.

https://originstutoring.lpages.co/act-aspire-math-grade-3/

Thank you for selecting this book.

We would be thrilled if you left us a review on the website where you bought this book!

www.ingramcontent.com/pod-product-compliance
Lightning Source LLC
Chambersburg PA
CBHW081348080526
44588CB00016B/2413